# ENGLISH FOR TOMORROW

**Open University Press**

English, Language, and Education series

*General Editor*: Anthony Adams
Lecturer in Education, University of Cambridge

SELECTED TITLES IN THE SERIES

# ENGLISH FOR TOMORROW

**Sally Tweddle**
**Anthony Adams**
**Stephen Clarke**
**Peter Scrimshaw**
**Shona Walton**

Open University Press
*Buckingham* • *Philadelphia*

Open University Press
Celtic Court
22 Ballmoor
Buckingham
MK18 1XW

and

1900 Frost Road, Suite 101
Bristol, PA 19007, USA

First Published 1997

*PE
66
.E64
1997*

A catalogue record of this book is available from the British Library

ISBN 0 335 19780 9 (pbk.)

**Library of Congress Cataloging-in-Publication Data**

English for tomorrow / Sally Tweddle . . . [et al.].
    p.   cm.
   Includes bibliographical references and index.
   ISBN 0–335–19780–9 (pbk.)
   1. English philology—Study and teaching—Technological
innovations.  2. English philology—Study and teaching—Data
processing.  3. Information technology.  I. Tweddle, Sally, 1955–
PE66.E64  1997
428′.007—dc21                       96–54002
                                 CIP

Typeset by Graphicraft Typesetters Limited, Hong Kong
Printed in Great Britain by St Edmundsbury Press, Bury St Edmunds, Suffolk

To the memory of Jeremy,
friend and valued member
of the group

# Contents

# Acknowledgements

We would like to thank Nina Stone for her friendly and efficient support of the future English group, and NCET for funding and supporting much of the activity which has resulted in this book.

We would also like to thank the following for permission to use the following copyright material: Tara Mustapha for the story on pp. 31–3; Dorling Kindersley for the diagram reproduced on p. 55; Michael Tweddle for the diagram reproduced on p. 55; and Carol Rumens for the poem 'Star Whisper' on p. 78. Other illustrative material has kindly been provided by Sue Dymoke and by Bet Lowe and Redbridge LEA.

We apologize for any inadvertent omissions to this list of acknowledgements.

# List of contributors

**Editor writers**
A. Adams, Department of Education, University of Cambridge, UK
S. Tweddle, Institute for Cancer Studies, University of Birmingham, UK

**Core writers**
S. Clarke, School of Education, University of Leeds, UK
P. Scrimshaw, Centre for Language and Communications, The Open University, UK
S. Walton, Warwickshire Education Authority, UK

**Contributing writers**
C. Beavis, Faculty of Education, Deakin University, Australia
A. Goodwyn, School of Education, University of Reading, UK
L. Newlyn, St Edmund Hall, University of Oxford, UK
V. Prain, La Trobe University, Australia

**Reader writers**
S. Dymoke, West Bridgeford School, UK
B. Griffith, University of Calgary, Canada
P. Moore, British Telecom, UK
M. Schirali, Queen's University, Kingston, Canada
M. Spencer, Institute of Education, University of London, UK
D. Taverner, Department of Education, University of Cambridge, UK

Specific individual contributions are acknowledged by the insertion of the author's initials in bold after each contribution.

# General editor's introduction

One of the first volumes to be published in this series was Richard Knott's book, *The English Department in a Changing World* (1985). This attempted, relatively successfully in the context of its time, to address the question of what kind of English teaching was appropriate to the needs of students growing up in the 1980s. A short section of this book dealt with the newly emerging area of computers and English teaching and a great deal of its concern was with the new kinds of skills that would be needed when the generation of students currently in the schools entered the workplace. The challenge was how to prepare them for this world whilst keeping alive the humane traditions of English teaching.

The challenge for the writers of the present work has been a similar but a much more intractable one. There was no way at the time of writing *The English Department in a Changing World* that Richard could have foreseen the many changes that have taken place between its publication and the present time. Some of these changes, at least in England and Wales, have of course been political, with the introduction of the National Curriculum, the Report of the Cox Working Group, and the subsequent revisions of the National Curriculum for English under the successive administrations of the National Curriculum Council and the School Curriculum and Assessment Authority. No subject in the National Curriculum, including history, has been so politicized as English and the attempts to identify what school leavers ought to know, understand and be able to do in terms of English still continue. Many recent volumes in this series have sought to carry this debate further, notably Chris Davies' volume, *What is English Teaching?* (1996). Indeed, if one looks at the catalogue listing of the whole series, including the several volumes now out of print, one can see a clear conspectus of the way in which attitudes to English teaching have changed and continue to do so.

What we had not realized in terms of 1985 was how dramatically things were going to change in the world outside school and how rapid the process of change was going to be over a ten-year period although, with Esmor Jones,

I had made some attempts to explore this in an Open University Press book, not part of the series, entitled, *Teaching Humanities in the Microelectronics Age* (1983). The issues we began to explore there have been recurring themes, seen especially in Chandler and Marcus (1985) and Robinson (1985). It is significant that all of these books, dealing with the new technologies and English teaching, are now out of print. The world they explored has been overtaken by the change of events in this field.

The present volume is the outcome of the many discussions and experiments of the Futures English Working Group, established by the National Council for Educational Technology. However, as is apparent from the Foreword, the task that the Futures English group set itself was a daunting one: not so much to record and respond to the changes taking place in schools, but to forecast what might be the kind of world that would be the environment for a school leaver who had begun education by entering school in 1996. Hence what might seem the otherwise rather odd and fortuitous date of 2010 as the focus for our work. The thesis was that, although we could not hope to forecast accurately what the world would be like, especially in terms of technological development, we had a duty to attempt to discern what were likely to be the curriculum developments with which schools ought now to be engaging. I have been privileged to be a member of the NCET Futures English Working Group and am therefore a member of the main writing team that has produced this book, though none of the other members of the group should necessarily be assumed to be in agreement with the present introduction which, as usual, is written in my editorial capacity.

The group was much wider ranging than is suggested by the names listed on the cover. Major contributions, identified in their place, have been made in writing by other members of the group, but the volume has also been enhanced by discussions and contributions to the thinking of the group, both nationally and internationally, which have take place on a personal basis by face-to-face contact and also by various forms of electronic communication. The actual writing of the book took place remarkably quickly and this would certainly not have been possible if we had not made extensive use of the new technologies with which it deals.

But the book is essentially not about technology: it is about curriculum and curriculum change in response to changing circumstances, 'a changing world'. We have begun with the eternal issues that have been debated by English teachers ever since the subject first began, long before it had established a bridgehead in the schools, such issues as the nature of text and how people engage with, interpret and construct texts of all kinds and for all manner of purposes. It is the context that has changed rather than the fundamentals of our task and craft.

I believe therefore that the present volume has many places where it should find resonances with the work currently going on in schools and with practices that can take place without an excessive use of the new technologies themselves. Several of the case studies in Chapter 4 point to this and, even the 'future-gazing' of the final chapter is firmly rooted in the here and now, in what is already possible, though perhaps not yet common, practice in the schools. However it does chart some of the directions in which we think English teaching should move if we are to meet the needs of the pupil leaving school in the year 2010, a hypothesis when we began our work but now a reality already present in the schools. This is especially important as an activity at the present time, given that the existing National Curriculum, post-Dearing, is to remain in force until the year 2000: already we need to be considering what should be the parameters of the curriculum which will succeed it. In many ways, especially in English, it could be argued that the present curriculum is backwards looking, more a curriculum for the nineteenth than the twentieth century; the need now to lay the foundations for the English curriculum of the twenty-first century becomes paramount.

Given that I have already been able to make my contribution to the book through the work of the Futures English group this introduction should be relatively brief. It does also, however, mark the end of an era which demands some comment in its own right. Since Richard Knott's book, mentioned earlier, until the present day, the series to which this book belongs has numbered, in all, 52 volumes. The time has now come for the series to come to an end and this will be the last book to appear under the series title, *English, Language, and Education*. I have greatly enjoyed the task of being the series editor. As we reach its close I would like to take the opportunity of thanking all my many contributing authors and I am very conscious of the memories of those who have died since they made their contributions. I would like to personally dedicate not just this final volume, but the series as a whole, to their vision and their memory.

*Anthony Adams*

# Foreword

This book is the culmination of a programme of work initiated by the National Council for Educational Technology (NCET) in 1992. Its aim was to develop a vision of the future of learning with information technology – of what, when and how we learn and how that is changing with information technology. The first step was to undertake a review of 39 texts recommended by experts in the field and comprising empirical evidence, professional views and visions of futurologists (see Appendix 2 for the list of texts). Subsequently, two national invitational seminars were held to initiate a debate about the future curriculum. Delegates were invited from education, industry and business; within education all sectors, phases and most curriculum areas were represented. The 1993 report on the literature review and the seminars concluded with some key questions for English:

- What is a useful meta-language for talking about texts which include print, non-print and information technology texts?
- What are the skills, knowledge and understandings which are required for reading with information technology texts?
- How do we teach children to become critical readers and writers of information technology texts?
- How can we use information technology to provide a range of authentic purposes for work in English?
- How does the increase in the use of graphics within texts affect what pupils write and the way they write it?

In order to focus more closely on the implications of such questions for the future English curriculum and for its assessment, in November 1993 NCET brought together a number of English specialists for an invitational seminar. Articles and papers, which included the 'Future curriculum with information technology' report, were distributed as background reading. The starting point for the seminar was a consideration of two key questions:

- In 2010 what should children of 11 know, understand and be able to do with information technology in English?
- In 2010 what will be an appropriate examination in English at age 18?

The discussions ranged widely and we recognized that as a group we could make only a small contribution to an area that was growing in importance. Indeed, as we have shared ideas with others in Britain and elsewhere, we have become ever more aware of the amount and quality of thinking that is currently taking place and of the narrowness of the field we have managed to cover. Nevertheless, the thinking that took place in that first seminar has underpinned the work that separately and together we have gone on to do, and the teachers and academics with whom we have shared our developing ideas have been overwhelmingly positive about its value.

During the first half of 1994, while battles were waged over the rewriting of the National Curriculum for English, a subset of the seminar participants continued to meet to develop the thinking of the first meeting and to identify small-scale research activities which would inform our work. From the summer of 1994 until April 1995, NCET part-funded three small research projects, which are continuing as we write, and the findings of which have fed into this book. They were:

- working with primary teachers in Redbridge LEA to learn more about reading and the teaching of reading with CD-ROMs (see Chapter 4, pp. 70–1);
- examining the attitudes of trainee English teachers to information technology and information technology texts (see Chapter 3, pp. 60–3);
- reviewing the literature on collaborative writing as a basis for developing models for the new types of collaboration enabled by information technology (Chapters 2 and 3).

While the research was under way we began talking more widely about our thinking, spending 1995 giving talks and seminars, developing INSET activities and attending conferences. Of particular significance was the conference of the International Federation for the Teaching of English (IFTE) held in New York in July 1995, for it was there that we came to see how widely accepted was the imperative to rethink English for the twenty-first century (we say more about the conference in Chapter 3). Early in September 1995 a joint seminar brought together council members, chief executives, members of senior management and curriculum officers from NCET and SCAA (the Schools Curriculum and Assessment Authority) to examine the implications of information technology for the future curriculum. The Introduction to this book was provided by NCET as pre-reading alongside papers from other curriculum areas; it was an attempt to identify the issues which will need to be addressed over the next few years if the teaching of English is ultimately to change in the ways that we are suggesting in this book.

This book is the final formal commitment for the NCET English Future Curriculum Group. The process of producing it has itself taken our thinking forward: in writing with the new technologies about writing with the new technologies we have learned at first hand what we needed to write. We hand the manuscript over on 1 September 1996 and will see the book in print for June 1997. That will be five years from the time when NCET's 'Vision' team started its work. The following five years will take us firmly into the twenty-first century. It will call for courage then for us to look back on what we are writing now, but whatever we may have failed to foresee, we believe that there will be much in this book that will still hold true.

# Introduction

**New technologies will not invalidate existing reasons for learning to read and write**

- Reading gives access to knowledge, literary heritage, culture, individual expression and argument.
- Writing enables groups and individuals to articulate and reform knowledge, express themselves and develop arguments.
- Literacy is necessary for effective functioning at work and in society.
- Both reading and writing give pleasure and personal fulfilment.

Reading is informed by understanding where texts come from and who has written them, how they are made and why they are made. Writing their own texts helps pupils to develop that understanding.

**New technologies do extend what there is to learn**

The question for English is how the subject might change in order to accommodate a growing body of knowledge and skills.

**New technologies for reading and writing have extended the curriculum for English**

Students now need opportunities to understand:

- how the use of word processors, spell checkers and thesauruses affects the processes involved in the different stages of composition and presentation of text;
- how the research opportunities offered by CD-ROM and Internet-based services can be used to support the study of literature and language;

- how the use of electronic sources of information can enhance the processes of comparison and synthesis of information drawn from different texts;
- how use of the Internet extends and changes possibilities for communicating with, and publishing for, real audiences across the world.

### New kinds of texts and textual practices create new areas of learning for the future

The use of multimedia[1] and electronic communications[2] is proliferating in the worlds of work, home and school. The texts generated with them reach different audiences and fill a function which is distinct from those of books and other print, from television and from film. Learning about and working with the implications of this is a potential new area of study for English students.

The new texts:

- include pictures and sound as well as words;
- are fluid and temporary, like, for example, texts on the World Wide Web,[3] which can be changed and made to connect differently with other texts;
- offer differing degrees of interactivity, as with animated books and interactive video;
- offer immediacy of feedback and informality, as with electronic mail, which encourages a compressed, informal style of communication that is somewhere between speech and writing;
- use different structures and conventions, such as hypertexts[4] which are not linear like books, or electronic mail;
- are published in different forms, such as CD-ROM encyclopaedias;
- are disseminated through different routes and for different audiences, as were the accounts of their experiences published on the Internet by Japanese children after their experience of the Kobe earthquake.

A fundamental question for the English curriculum of the future will be how these 'new' texts are used to express ideas that could not be expressed through 'older' texts.

In many ways the skills and knowledge required to read and write such texts are unchanged from those required by the older kinds of texts. However, there will be a need for a broader repertoire of analytical skills and expanded criteria to enable students to make decisions about reading and writing based upon their understanding of what different texts are good for.

### Reading

Readers of new texts will need to be able to determine whether the image, the sound or the word is the principal carrier of meaning in any text: most literate adults today still assume that images are used to 'illustrate' the main message, which is conveyed through words. Students will need to understand the inter-action of words, pictures and sound and recognize and interpret ambiguities created by that interaction.

Children will apply what they learn about spoken English to help them 'read' sounds in multimedia texts. They will also need to know how non-verbal sounds function in electronic texts.

As they do today, students will need to be able to establish a text's proven-ance – where it comes from and what its status and validity are. With computer texts this is particularly important: children who do not know that these texts are written by 'authors' accord them a degree of authority and impartiality that they do not possess.

## Writing

Writers will need to understand the strengths and weaknesses of the new forms of text and their appropriateness for particular purposes and audiences. This will require them to broaden their understandings about texts in relation to:

- the medium in which they are represented (e.g. multimedia, language, sound, image);
- the mode of transmission (e.g. print, electronic, handwriting, spoken);
- the form (e.g. e-mail discussion, scripted drama, hypertext).

Pupils are already editing, copying, cutting and pasting with words. With 'new' texts they might well be offered the opportunity to learn how to do the same with pictures and sound. How classroom time might be given to addressing this issue raises a question, among others, about the usual separation within the curriculum of art and music from English.

With the advent of opportunities to collaborate in different ways and with different people, students will need to know how to decide which types of col-laboration to adopt on which occasions. An increase in the opportunities for col-laborative writing will raise questions for teachers of how to assess individual achievement.

## Conclusion

Electronic communications create new opportunities for readers and writers; multimedia brings together word, moving image and sound. Together they provide new means for the representation and communication of meaning. It seems improbable that electronic texts will ever threaten the primacy of the printed word but it is already evident that the balance between the two is changing. How the English curriculum can reflect this changing situation will be a key question for the next century.

## Source

Internal discussion document. National Council for Educational Technology, September 1995.

## Notes

1 Texts which include words, moving images and sound.
2 Fax, electronic mail, video conferencing etc.
3 An international database of hypermedia texts which can be read by users of the Internet.
4 Texts in which certain words or pictures are linked to other pages; the result is a non-linear structure of pages which can be reached by a number of different routes.

# 1     The context for English

As long ago as 1981 the Open University Press published *The Future of the Printed Word* (Hills, 1981). This was a symposium collection of articles by 14 writers exploring the continuing role of the printed word in an age of increasing electronic communication. The opening chapter by John Strawborn of the Vitro Laboratories Division of Automation Industries, USA, concluded:

> Our challenge . . . will be to exploit the rapidly evolving hardware to present new and improved types of software . . . to provide people with the information they want and need, at the proper time, in the proper form, wherever they need it.
>
> The creation and dissemination of the printed word will continue to be part art, part engineering. If we pursue it diligently and intelligently, we will improve the engineering and extend it into areas as yet barely touched on, and we will do so without losing the art. We may even advance it.

In the near 15 years since this was written, the 'engineering' has developed considerably and in many directions that could not have been foreseen in 1981; the 'art' remains much as it was then. In the field of education and schooling in particular the hopes that were raised initially by the development of the Microelectronics Education Programme (MEP), announced by the government in March 1980, have been shown to have been largely illusory.

The programme started with excellent intentions. In April 1981 its director, Richard Fothergill wrote:

> The aim of the Programme is to help schools to prepare children for life in a society in which devices and systems based on microelectronics are commonplace and pervasive. These technologies are likely to alter the relationships between one individual and another and between individuals and their work; and people will need to be aware that the speed of change is accelerating and that their future careers may well involve retraining stages as they adjust to new technological developments.
>
> (Fothergill, 1981)

However, despite the investment in hardware and software that followed, teaching and learning fifteen years later have not changed much as a consequence. It is the premise of this book that the changes enabled and driven by technology have become so far-reaching that for English teachers to ignore them would prove ultimately irresponsible. This chapter gives an overview of these changes and suggests that there are forces already in place which require a reconsideration of the subject 'English'.

## Changing technologies

Outside the schoolroom, the impact of the new technologies is very different today from what it was even five years ago. The penetration into the home of the computer, increasingly in the form of fully fledged multimedia systems, has been ever accelerating and unstoppable, so that some children are arriving in schools at the age of 5 already taking the so-called 'new technologies' as much for granted as the video-recorder that, once a luxury, is now to be found in almost every British home. The latest social trends statistics do not even note how many video-recorders there are, given their ubiquity, more so in fact than the telephone. It is our contention that this existing penetration into the home of the microcomputer is significant for the future of schooling, especially in the field of English, for the technological revolution with which we are concerned has been primarily associated with the extension of our conception of text (printed, spoken, written and electronic) and the range of information that this has made available to us. The thesis that underlies all that follows is that we need to refine and redefine our concept of texts and how we use them in schooling, so as to take account of the changes that have taken place in the home lives of many of our pupils, whether they have access to computers or not. One of the issues that will also need to be addressed is the question of equity, as computers become more widely used in society and, at the same time, more accessible to a larger proportion of the population. We will need to ensure that pupils from a wide range of backgrounds all have access to the necessary technology to develop their skills in and understanding of what is in many ways a new literacy.

In the past we have not shown ourselves to have been very good at taking seriously the learning that is required by new technologies. Although television is the main means of information and cultural transmission in our society, and there is some excellent media studies practice, we still do too little about it in most of our schools. As a consequence we fail to build upon the highly developed visual literacy of our pupils. If schooling is to remain significant into the next century, as we believe it should, we must do better with the more recent technologies than we have done with television, not least because there is a fundamental difference between them. In the case of television, it can be argued that viewing is often a solitary activity. Many young people now have televisions in their own rooms so that they can view programmes of their own choice as and when they want to.

Even so, television viewing can also be a social activity. Buckingham and Sefton-Green (1993) have shown how adolescents frequently 'get together' to watch some types of videos, especially violent ones. Both they and adults rent a video as they would go to the cinema, so that, in such cases, viewing becomes a domestic and social event. We probably need to make a clear distinction between television viewing and the viewing of videos; for another fundamental difference between them is that, with the video, the user has greater control. It is the user who decides how much is to be watched and when; there is the opportunity to rewind, to freeze frame, to speed up or slow down. In both respects the video has much more in common with the social interactivity of some computer programs than with the much more sedentary activity of the less easily controlled medium of television.

Because the child's home computer may well end up in the bedroom along-side the television set, attention has been focused on the fact that it may encourage some forms of solitary activity, such as the playing of addictive computer games. But it is potentially a *social* medium: in the bedroom doing their home-work pupils can now communicate via the Internet with their peers; the work that they do can become (perhaps more often than their teachers appreciate) the result of a collaborative process. The irony is that this kind of collaborative communication is made possible through the older medium of the telephone. Arguably the telephone has, like the television, led primarily (in spite of the potential of teleconferencing) to one-to-one communication. Yet when Alexander Bell invented the telephone he thought that he was inventing something more like broadcasting: a means of transmitting something over a distance to a room full of people. Now, what he had in mind is made much more achievable through the combination of his invention with the increasingly affordable and portable computer. The potential of collaborative communication, among teachers and students, and its implication for English teaching, is one of the issues with which this book will be primarily concerned.

The extent to which social interaction is encouraged or enabled by the use of computers is an important issue with major pedagogical implications, and depends upon decisions made by teachers and administrators. Much of the early literature about the use of computers in schools stressed their value in collaborative work (Chandler and Marcus, 1985; Robinson, 1985). But, with hindsight, this can now be seen as a function of the scarcity of the hardware. The basic tradition of the English classroom is based upon individualistic patterns of learning and success predicated on individual achievement. Such an approach contrasts strongly with the use of computers and the way they have been more recently introduced in Japanese classrooms, as reported by a Cambridge doctoral student, Bryn Holmes (1997). Her classroom observation in roughly comparable classrooms in Britain and Japan shows that in the British classrooms most teachers expect pupils to work quietly on their own.

The teachers' ideal would be to have each pupil working at a single computer station. There is thus little direct encouragement of collaborative work. (The strong interest that has been shown in the use of integrated learning systems is a further indication of this trend.)

In the observed Japanese classrooms, even though there was no shortage of hardware, pupils invariably worked in pairs at a computer terminal and there was a constant babble of talk as pupils helped each other in their work. The British classroom was individualistic; the Japanese one was essentially collaborative. The classrooms were clearly revealing profound differences in the two societies, which are later carried through into the workplace and attitudes to work.

## Changing texts

Changing technologies generate changing texts. It has frequently been remarked that Socrates regarded the invention of writing as a potential danger to learning, as written text obviated the need for memory. Thus all new technological developments are at first viewed with suspicion, since they disturb the accepted conventions which preceded them. The epic poem, with such devices as the stock epithet, developed its particular structure because of the need for it to be memorized by a succession of bards and rhapsodists. Yet even then, each generation of tellers sought to challenge the limits of the rhetoric available to it. Part of the direction the growth of literary form has taken developed from this tension between the accepted and received modes and the challenges brought to bear upon them by innovators. It was precisely here that the genius of Shakespeare was to be seen in the challenge he presented to the conventions of the theatre of his day.

In the same way that the bard and the dramatist challenged, and were challenged by, the prevailing verbal and theatrical conventions, the innovator in the age of print, which has dominated Western culture for the past 450 years, has sought to push beyond its boundaries. Some of the most striking examples of this can be seen in the work of Lawrence Sterne, William Blake, Emily Brontë, James Joyce, Virginia Woolf and many others. More recently, we have seen the rise of the graphic novel, which has again challenged our assumptions about print technology, as can be seen in the adaptation of the picture book format to the adult 'novel', as in Raymond Briggs's tale of nuclear war, *Where the Wind Blows*.

If we ask what is characteristic of the physical structure of the printed word as it is to be found in conventional books, it is its sequential nature; that is, books are printed with pages bound in a particular order. This structure encourages, though it does not force, an expectation that the text is to be read in the order in which it is bound. However, this is not necessarily always what authors intend.

We can distinguish two distinct approaches here. One is embodied in such contemporary genres as the magazine and the newspaper, where linear reading is not envisaged. Indeed, with the physically segmented supplements in the Sunday papers, we see how the emphasis upon the reader choosing what to read has carried over into a break-up of the physical unity of the text. Similarly, such well known genres as the pocket tourist guide, the encyclopaedia and the dictionary illustrate that neither a linear reading nor a complete reading of texts needs to be automatically assumed even in the case of bound books.

Alongside that stands the tradition of the narrative text or, more widely, of literary fiction. Such texts are usually to be read from the beginning until the end, as Lewis Carroll, another innovator, reminds us in *Alice in Wonderland*: ' "Begin at the beginning," the King said, gravely, "and go on till you come to the end; then stop." ' Carroll, however, also shows himself to be aware of some of the other aspects of text that may be more in our consciousness as we think of multimedia presentation, for, in the same text, Alice remarks: 'What is the use of a book without pictures or conversations?' It is significant that here, as so often, Alice, the child, shows herself much more aware than the adults who surround her and seek to patronize her.

Such a sequential pattern of reading is not necessarily the only option with texts that are published via the medium of computers, as Myron Tuman (1992) maintains in what he calls 'the new reading':

> When we read a loosely structured literary work like Whitman's *Leaves of Grass* . . . we are given a path to follow image by image, line by line, stanza by stanza, poem by poem throughout the entire text. When we work with this same volume on-line, searching backward and forward following the trail of images and illusions [*sic*] that interest us (even using nothing more powerful than a simple word processing program), the entire nature of the reading process is transformed. *Leaves of Grass* changes from a set of poems with an extended linear sequence established by the author to a computer database, a collection of information stored in one form by the author (or compiler) but accessed by the reader in another.

The implications of this comment (of which, we think, Whitman would have been approving), both for literary study and for our understanding of the nature of text, are an important consideration of this book. Far from linearity being the 'natural' way of viewing texts, it is but one of many possible ways of conceiving the relationship between the physical and conceptual structure of texts that an author may have. A preference for non-linear readings has been important, and arguably dominant, in popular writing in this century, and has been a source of opportunity for experiment by a minority of fiction writers too, as well as some of the major ones already mentioned. Non-linearity can also be found in the work of such children's authors as Alan Sharp in his development of the popular form of the branching story, seen in the Cambridge University Press series, *Storytrails*. What the new technologies have made possible is not the creation of a new kind of text that no one until now has really wanted to create or read. Rather, these hypertexts represent a technical way to achieve what many writers have always seen in the printed word alone as an obstacle to the production of the kind of texts they wished to develop.

In this connection it is interesting to note the decision in 1995 of the well established publisher of children's reference books, Dorling Kindersley, to switch into publishing through the medium of CD-ROM. Given the highly visual nature of the reference books they have traditionally published, it is clear that they saw in the new medium now becoming widely available something that would better enable them to achieve their objectives. They must also have seen it as a wise economic decision given the direction the production of reference materials was taking. Such a choice would not, of course, have been available to them without the wide opening up at that time of the home market in terms of multimedia computer systems. As always, whatever form of publication is engaged in will be subject to economic and social constraints alongside technical ones.

The computer, therefore, allows a novelist an expansion of possibilities which are comparable in scale and significance to that which writers for the proscenium theatre experienced when drama was first transferred to the new medium of film. The effects that film script writers were to achieve with the tracking shot and the close-up were things that, no doubt, any playwright would have valued, had the physical structure of the theatre allowed him or her to envisage such possibilities. The same expansion of possibilities is the case with the move from the printed to the electronic word.

## Changing literacy practice

The traditional emphasis upon linearity as a way of reading a text is highly vulnerable. It is not the case that readers (at least at the level of paragraph and sentence reading) track through a text in a strict sequence which is defined solely by the order of the words on the page. Rather, they dart backwards and forwards across the text, building up the meaning by references forward and back as they go. There may be some cases where both reader and writer envisage reading a novel as a linear process, working from each chapter to the next. Indeed, some genres (notably the whodunnit) depend heavily upon such an assumption. However, this is to take a distinctly limited view of what constitutes reading. Evocation and references forward and back are part of the writer's craft, whether embodied in such large-scale devices as the flashback (something as old as Homer) or in the more subtle details of a sentence that recalls an earlier one in some way. Writers use these techniques to recognize and support the reader's tendency to construct a reading not simply from the text on a single page, but through unconscious reference, both cognitive and emotional, to earlier passages in the text and also by explicit or implied reference to other texts. Reading is not a mechanical march through a prestructured text but more of a negotiated construction of meaning in which both reader and writer actively participate. (For an illuminating and fuller discussion of this see Iser, 1978.) What the new technology allows is a wider range of freedoms within which this transaction between author and reader may be conducted.

Another example of changing literary practices is the composition of the present text. In the book by Hills quoted in the opening sentence of this chapter it was mentioned that that work was a compilation of chapters by 14 contributors; the present volume has been crafted by many more than this. Yet each individual chapter has no single author; each has been worked over by a number of writers and readers from around the world. In this sense the work is itself an example of the kind of collaboration which has been made possible by the new technology and in a way which we see as central to the concerns of education at the turn of the century.

Much has been made of the idea of multiple authorship and shared composition in the growing body of rhetoric concerning information technology and texts, reading and the subject 'English' (see, for example, Montieth, 1993). The 'old' technologies do not in themselves prevent sharing, and the realization of some art forms, such as opera, relies upon careful cooperation between a large number of people, each acting creatively, with different roles and talents. However, plays, poems and novels usually have single names attached to them, and in the case of opera, credit consistently goes to a single composer for the inspiration, if not the realization, of the work. Despite the traditional nature of some kinds of shared creative activities, however, the new possibilities for making shared authorship on a daily basis much more possible are such that we need to consider further questions of origin, participation and form, as we shall do in Chapter 2.

The inspiration/realization distinction begins to lose its neatness when the technologies by which works are produced can cancel the old time gaps and when the finished product can be previewed in its virtual 'final' form. For example, we have traditionally expected musical ideas to come from the composer and visual ideas (the correlatives of the music) to come from the director and the designer. The two sets of ideas thus have a quasi-hierarchical relationship. There may not be such a clear separation or hierarchy in the future, if, for example, the composer sketches designs for staging and sets on the same computer as that which is being used to compose the musical score. One could activate or animate the other in ways which a creative mind could find very persuasive. What also if a composer needed help with design or a designer help with the music? The fluidity of the computing medium, combined with its capacity to store so many images for borrowing and adaptation, could enable new forms of 'composing'. Perhaps music and libretto could be worked on almost simultaneously between composer and poet, with the designer tuning in to words and sound, and able to extend and modify these in their embryonic stages. The singers could also be in on the act at an early stage, by pointing out to the poet the difficulty of sustaining high notes on certain vowel sounds, and thus the verbal score could be adapted to their needs, or the poet could ask the composer to alter the musical line so that the original words remained. All this will, of course, call for new skills in negotiation between the collaborating 'authors' that will make the battles between Gilbert and Sullivan in their differences over the composition of the Savoy Operas a mere bagatelle.

The potential for such plasticity in the process of creation is even more pronounced when we recognize that those taking part in the process need not be physically contingent to each other but may be sharing their ideas (verbal, musical, pictorial) by means of electronic communication.

This is all very speculative about the relationship of the form of the finished product to a future process of composition, and we need to remember that, as at present, some things will continue to begin in unique minds and require other minds to free them into life on a later occasion.

### Changing content

Just as changing technologies bring about changes in texts, so too they ought to bring about changing contents and contexts for schooling. Earlier in this chapter we referred to the impact of television on society, but its relative, and continuing, neglect in school. Video, usually of television programmes, is now extensively used as a teaching aid, or even employed instead of teaching in some instances, but the 'use' can be very simplistic. The 'material' is used generally because it is seen as being more up to date and more exciting than the contents of the relevant textbook. It is rarely mediated by the teacher. This reveals, among other things, the conservatism of most schools and of much teaching. The new material is simply subsumed into the school subject and the subject, traditionally, carries on.

Practice in some English lessons is a good deal more challenging and critical than the above, but television itself as a medium is too rarely examined. Equally, newspapers are made considerable use of, but few departments have a unit of work which explores the functions and power of the popular press and magazines. Pupils endlessly churn out 'newspaper articles' as part of their writing repertoire but with no sense that they are building up a capacity to be more effective, critical citizens in an age when anyone might genuinely contribute to the host of local and national newspapers.

All this suggests an implicit assumption that the school should be preserved as a place free from the vulgarities of popular culture. It is fine to use the material generated by the modern media as illustrative material, but not to engage with it or its means of production.

The way in which many English teachers make use of the media also reminds us of the English teachers' traditional training as critic rather than as practitioner or artist. This limitation was one of the things which gave rise to the early aridity of media studies in schools. The same convention applied in both the subject areas of English and media studies; that is, if you produced something you had to justify it with a critical commentary. In media studies especially, the thing produced could only be considered as an inferior imitation of a 'real' media product.

The process of critical commentary is not itself in question and is perfectly valuable for many reasons. However, the boundaries will soon disappear between the 'original' and the 'imitation'. It is already possible to capture and re-edit everything from Gilbert and Sullivan to the nine o'clock news. What will this mean?

First, it will not mean a glorious new dawn where anyone in society can use anything; there is too much money in the control of copyright for that. However, it may mean that, in schools, the English classroom will finally justify that much overused word, 'workshop'.

Second, pupils will be able to bring in, from their home machines, disks containing all kinds of 'meanings'. These can be meanings from any of the media, whether captured, scanned in or created at home. Such meanings will also be fluid and open to endless interpretation and reinterpretation. Who owns them will be problematic. Such proliferation of meaning will be neither better nor worse than current practice unless thinking makes it so. What we will have, however, will be a different kind of opportunity to blend the creative and the critical.

Children, in the majority of homes, together with their English teachers, are likely to have access to hundreds of thousands of stored programmes, films, archives of newspapers, sound recordings of all kinds, print texts and still images. Making sense of all this will continue to become more difficult unless teachers, in the best traditional sense, offer guidance and ask the right questions. The teachers will need to know more than at present about the production, history, storage and ownership of visual and verbal texts and to relish the possibilities of infinite reproduction and interpretation. They will need to see a book for what it is, an object made by a machine and a team of people, sold to make someone (rarely the author) rich. Implicit in the object they will see, instead of the unique, almost sacred author's manuscript, the text's essential plasticity: its capability of being transformed in endless variations.

An art form which was created by an earlier 'new technology', the film, is an example of this. Films may begin in unique minds, like those of Hitchcock, and may take on a special resonance through their maker, but in most cases we link single names to them with less ease and less readiness than we do to plays. Perhaps films share something in compositional terms with an art form whose rise accompanied theirs, namely jazz. Their structure relies on a great deal more than improvisation alone, but some of the freshness and ebullience of the early silent comedy films looks as if they sprang from a ready willingness to share and to experiment, to use whatever was to hand in the environment to help a comic idea take on greater proportions of the absurd. Who made which decisions, in terms of the finished product, out there on the early film lots?

The fact that this question can never be answered raises significant questions of ownership which become ever more pressing as we provide the possibilities of such collaborative work in the arts and in our schools. How, for example, will teachers make judgements about the achievement of pupils who are learning to write collaboratively; indeed, how many of today's and tomorrow's teachers have themselves engaged in collaborative writing and what models of collaboration have they been using?

Such questions as this have important implications for the future education of teachers. As long ago as 1965, Charles Hannam of the University of Bristol School of Education lamented that we still train teachers on 'the assumption that they will lead solitary lives' (Hannam, 1965). Can such an assumption be valid today, as the once impregnable walls of the classroom give way to the 'virtual reality' classroom? On 16 February 1996, for example, the BBC1 programme *Tomorrow's World* presented an item about a virtual classroom in the Arctic Circle where 'schools' in remote areas got together with a specialist teacher of a specific subject linked by computers and video so that they could all cooperate in teaching and learning together. This was essentially different from conventional distance learning in the opportunity provided for the encouragement of interaction between the pupils, who were able to learn from and, in some ways, to experience each other's lifestyles. Though this was an expedient developed to meet a particular need, the potential it provides could be extended elsewhere and the programme made clear that this was intended to happen in some other Scandinavian countries.

The film makers, like the jazz musicians, were free of classical rules, and this allowed them to say things that others, working in traditional forms, had neither the wish nor the means to say, and, in doing so, to shape popular tastes as much as simply to follow the compulsions of a market. They were also pioneering the possibilities of a new form. In a sense they were acting as some of the earliest novelists had acted, where the lack of the right kind of education disbarred them from attempting the epic, the tragic or comic staged play, or the properly revered forms of verse. Deborah Cameron's (1990) thesis about how women came to write novels because they were free to experiment with a new form that lacked classical precedents, and thus status, and so also the entire set of critical and corrective constraints of those precedents, has relevance here. Of course, in terms of the novel, as well as the film, the emergence of new readerships and new forms coincided with the emergence of new economic structures and social orders.

It may well be that there is a kind of parallel here between the advent of the film makers and the jazz musicians, and that of the digital technologies which will come to shape so many of what we will in time come to accept as new expressive forms. Quite what a computer will be like in a few years time is hard to guess – and any guess is almost certain to prove wrong. However, it seems relatively safe to predict that the next generation of computers will enable each of us to improvise with combinations of pictures, speech, text and music, and to share our thinking in ways that have not been easily possible until recently. Once television stations alone had the technology to create televisual images, but we can now do that at a popular level with the use of camcorders. In its various forms, including the employment of digital cameras to feed material into hypercard presentations, the visual will come to be a very readily available medium for the exploration of expressive ideas, as well as for the transmission of information. However, this is by no means to say that there will be a rush into visual links for all purposes. Many of us would prefer telephone calls to go on revealing only what our voices give away and would not want a camera to show us speaking on the telephone on all occasions. There is nothing sinister or impolite about this, it is simply a cultural adaptation to a medium. However, the more such media become available to us and the more we have to make choices between them, the more important such cultural adaptations will become.

Pioneer work on the implications of the visual for English teaching has been done by Richard Andrews (1996), who has classified how much, at a daily level, of what we read and absorb is accompanied by pictures and sound. Children are growing up learning to read, much as they have done for a hundred years, but, though in school many texts remain print dominated, few arrive from the home without the accompaniment of coloured pictures. Kress (1995) makes a powerful case through a few selected pieces of evidence to the effect that, even in schools, informational texts have a predominately visual format, with ideas conveyed through pictures, and that this is now the expected norm. No longer are illustrations the mere accompaniment to the explanation of a concept which is given through words; pictures have become the basic vehicle for explanatory work.

Possibilities for the digitally based creating and communicating of our ideas and experiences have yet to be refined, extended, sub-divided and enriched, but it does not seem like naive optimism to suggest that they will be. In one very obvious sense we shall, in order to claim to be well educated, have to understand more than we generally do at present about the communicative choices available to us and about what forms as well as what media are most appropriate at a given moment. Our pupils will need to be both craftspersons and artists, well versed in literacy skills at a number of levels. Perhaps the reason why explanations about electric motors are now provided more by illustration than by printed text has to do with the perceptual skills of most of us, who find it hard to visualize where the electricity is going, and what it does, from print alone. But how much clearer would the workings of such motors be if their descriptions were in the form of text, together with voice-over, accompanied by an interactive illustration on screen, with labelling and help bubbles at the click of a cursor and a moving diagrammatic representation which could be viewed from any angle using computer graphics, the speed of which could be controlled by the twitch of a mouse?

To be able to follow such illustrations and graphics, with the right kind of concentration and understanding, is as important a skill of the new literacy as following the words. Reading a poem, however, will remain primarily an encounter with words and their arrangement on the page. This in itself, of course, can also be a visual and multimedia experience as is seen in poems as diverse as Herbert's 'Easter Wings', Carroll's 'Mouse's Tail', and Morgan's 'Message Clear'.

We hope that English teachers will continue to teach ways in which poems can become important events inside our own heads, as well as part of the fleeting semantics of a tube-train journey. Perhaps, however, English lessons can consign vivid word accounts of bonfire night to the bonfires themselves, because if we want vividness of actuality rather than formless ritualized lists of present participles, then the students can capture it on video, and face the problems of editing in order to create some kind of meaning. The editing will be done on a computer, by groups, and by the time the pupils have finished they will probably have written more (and certainly talked more), with a better sense of what the writing had to do with the sights and sounds they experienced, than they would have done under the old order. One might not be able to call such an editing exercise 'shaping at the point of utterance', but 'uttering at the point of re-shaping' may prove powerful in bringing elements of aesthetic awareness to consciousness. English teaching will need to continue to be about that.

## A changing world

There are forces in place which could easily influence the future of English teaching. Gunther Kress, in his monograph *Writing the Future: English and the Making of a Culture of Innovation* (1995), makes a determined plea for a radical re-casting of English, one that is aware of the rapidity of the changes in the world in which our children will have to live, and in which they will strive to enjoy satisfying and fulfilling lives. English will remain a core subject because of its concern with individual identity and with the means whereby we come to understand who we are. However, the construction of this individual identity is very far removed from the subjectivities celebrated in earlier versions of English. In order to understand how you signify as an individual, you need, according to Kress, to understand the nature of the texts around you, be they culturally salient texts, aesthetically revered texts or mundane ones. How far a stress on cultural difference would help individuals to understand better the nature of their society, and thus the nature of their own identity, is uncertain. However, it could well be that schools will eventually catch up, in curriculum terms, with the choices pupils already make in terms of their appreciation of cultural diversity, utilizing those elements which seem most likely to provide scope for enjoyment and finding ways of incorporating them into new forms.

Fast capitalism, says Kress, shifts production and money around the globe as it pleases, and in so doing can play havoc with people's employment patterns. We could speculate that the new economic forces are going to have to find ways of accommodating rising demands for education and social justice. What if, for example, the major corporations agreed a contract with schools, to supply them with computers at the point at which they still worked perfectly well, but not as well as the latest generation machines? There is, after all, a possibility that the present pattern of dominance of the market by PCs could suddenly slip. For example, Simon Caulkin in *The Observer* (10 September 1995) speculated about the effects of a $400 Internet appliance which could plug into a wall anywhere and download on demand anything required, from video to audio to the latest word processing program. If businesses come to 'rent' computing power from the Net rather than to buy fleets of PCs then it could well be that the outdated machines could be given to schools before the chips are old. It would be a generosity coup, wonderful PR and, as a piece of pre-emptive tax avoidance, remarkably successful.

What we are suggesting here, through this speculative example, is that the political alliances between the government, the electorate and the corporations may yet tilt in favour of equipping schools properly. An English curriculum which is based on historical texts and critical procedures that are also traditional precludes the idea of development and an embracing of the future.

New areas within English, such as theatre studies and media studies at A level, continue to appear and to gain student numbers rapidly. Those engaged in training the next generation of English teachers are well aware that some areas of knowledge demanded by schools and the National Curriculum, such as awareness of the patterns and characteristic forms of spoken English, are utterly new ground to most English graduates. The forms of writing which are now required to be taught also comprise a wider set of genres than those studied within most literature-based English degrees.

In England, National Curriculum English is a version of the subject which greatly stresses the concept of the nation as enshrined in its literary heritage. When the forces of transnationalism threaten, as they do in much present-day economic and political activity, the official and controllable elements of the culture can be manipulated to reinforce the idea of cultural sovereignty and linguistic independence.

Programmes of study which include the area of language awareness can lead pupils to an understanding of what European languages have in common and enable them to make the most of the linguistic resources and understanding they already have to communicate with their fellow Europeans, since it is clearly never going to be possible for them to learn all the languages of the New Europe. Already text translation programs are available that make it possible for young learners to collaborate across national boundaries on projects such as environmental monitoring (Tilbury and Turner, 1996). It would seem an obvious extension for them to collaborate across national boundaries in studies involving media, language and literature.

Other countries, or at any rate those with a history of greater permeation by other cultures and languages, could suggest how a curriculum in literature might seek to discover the susceptibility of a single text, such as *Robinson Crusoe*, to be re-written across national boundaries and languages, as in *Swiss Family Robinson to Foe* by Coetzee performed by Theatre de Complicité. Other examples would be the Disney treatments of European fairy stories, or, with older students, a study of, say, the transformation of *Othello* into *Otello*. Such an approach could sustain the concept of literature as a central one for children to grasp by the time they left school, but the perspectives on that concept would be quite different from those offered around an essentially nation state view of literature, something which was there to reinforce commonality and stasis within boundaries rather than encourage evolution and adaptation across them.

It is not hard, then, to see that nothing should be presupposed as an unavoidable and absolute category when it comes to English teaching. The title of the subject does not in itself force its teachers to the conclusion that only texts which originated within England should be studied. The forms and nature of the English language can be studied in such a way as to suggest comparison with other languages at many points, so that similarities and differences became more subtly understood, and so that the idea of translation, with some attention to its specific difficulties, is also given at the same time as the study of the national tongue, or that which is the main one for most of the nation. (For a fuller discussion of this see Tulasiewicz and Adams, 1997.) Wherever we look in respect of the subject 'English', then, we can see that alternatives to the presently imposed curriculum suggest that a European perspective is not only available but would be positively advantageous. Shakespeare's plays are treated as if he were a national icon, a point discussed in Leach (1992), but the nature of their Europeanness, of their geographical settings and cross-border translations, is diminished in that iconic exploitation.

In the next few years, industry and commerce will become much less contained within national boundaries; workers will be encouraged to move between states in order to earn their living, as is envisaged in much European legislation since Maastricht. That in itself might well compel a revision of the concept of mother-tongue teaching across all national boundaries, and we have to note, within the remit of this book, that the increasing use of electronic communication systems could well aid that process. The teaching of modern foreign languages has already begun to explore the capacity of electronic links to enable students of different countries to explore together not just language issues, but cross-cultural ones too. However, this is only one kind of future gazing, partly inspired by the simple observation that significant numbers of postgraduate student teachers whose main subject is English end their courses determined to teach first in another country, or arrive on their course in teacher education already having gained experience abroad of teaching English as a foreign language.

We need, in the interests of extending the argument, to continue to bear in mind that Kress's emphases and perspectives are fairly radical. For example, they radically re-cast the notion of the authority of the text. If you take notes to holiday tenants as worthy of serious study (and a good case is made out for just that), then what becomes salient is not the power of the author, but the relationships of ordinary people to ordinary people and the linguistic terms of that relationship. Text analysis becomes societal analysis. English teaching in the future might well, therefore, become the beneficiary of the work of such theorists as Fairclough (1989). Socio-linguistics would at last have registered their place as central to the creation of a preparedness to resist informedly some of the more heavily mediated words and images.

The idea of a subject becoming both more radical and more democratic is one that Lanham (1993) links to developments in the electronic medium. His general point is that our ability to own massive corpora of texts on searchable formats and in changeable forms leaves us in less awe of a singular interpretive authority than we were in the days of print, not least because we can play with the texts as we wish. An interesting extension of Lanham's argument is that electronic verbal texts, with their mutability and media mixtures, return us to earlier rhetorical traditions in which style and voice are intimately part of the construction of meaning.

So, if the electronics allow a re-positioning of ourselves as readers and writers, and if Kress's insistence on seeing the relationships between the mundane and the revered as essentially non-hierarchical wins the day, and if English teachers incorporate a European dimension into their subject, what will happen to the subject 'English'? What will youngsters be taught to do, know and understand? It is to these questions that we address ourselves in this book, not with a certainty about our capacity to predict the detail of the future but with a broad brush approach that will enable us to represent the landscape into which we are moving as well as to focus in detail on some of the features of that landscape.

In the next chapter we look at reading and writing, at the significance for English teaching of what the new technologies have introduced into ways of working with texts and in relation to texts themselves. The third and central chapter presents a framework against which teachers can consider how they will respond both to the imperatives we have outlined here and to the new possibilities brought about by technology. We use this framework as a basis for teasing out, in our final two chapters, how present and future practice might look in relation to the basic issues which are the central concern of this book.

# 2 Writing and reading: texts and technologies

> The image of literature to be found in ordinary culture is tyrannically centred on the author, his person, his life, his tastes, his passions, while criticism still consists for the most part in saying that Baudelaire's work is the failure of Baudelaire the man, Van Gogh's his madness, Tchaikovsky's his vice. The explanation of a work is always sought in the man or woman who produced it, as if it were always in the end, through the more or less transparent allegory of the fiction, the voice of a single person, the author 'confiding' in us.
>
> (Barthes, 1977)

This notion of the relationship between author and text is, if Barthes is correct, one with which we are notionally all familiar and one which dominates most people's thinking about texts and their creators. In its most extreme form it sees literacy as centred upon the creation and understanding of single texts by individual authors through the single medium of writing or print. But is Barthes's account true today? There are other ways of looking at texts, which may be explicitly multiple-authored (as in the case of Gilbert and Sullivan, or when one author completes another's unfinished work as in the various proposed endings to Dickens's *The Mystery of Edwin Drood*); equally, a single author may produce a series of texts which are both complete in themselves and also interrelated in a complex way, such as Anthony Powell's novel sequence, *A Dance to the Music of Time*. By way of exemplification, let us consider a particular case, that of *Hamlet*, where the natural assumption might well be to see the work of art as a single text produced by a single author.

## Texts: *Hamlet*, single author, single text?

English teachers are familiar enough with problems of editing *Hamlet* and the varying possibilities which are opened up in making choices between, for example, the texts of the second Quarto of 1604/5 and the Folio of 1623, so that the singularity of the text is open for some debate and always has been.

Behind the variations, however, most of us have been led to feel that there does lie a 'true' version, the one and only finally intended edition whose exact shape may never be fully known, but which remains a distinct possibility should one day, perhaps, all editorial problems be resolved. Come that day we will know our hawks from our heronshaws, and there will be no more confusion of categories. This certainty, though, will be less likely to derive from historical empirics such as the discovery of a lost manuscript, and more likely to derive from interpretative editing that is more convincing than any previous editing; the concept of the singularly correct version drives the search and guides the interpretative critical acumen. A recent book by John Jones (1995) reinforces the view that it will be impossible to gain access to this 'true' *Hamlet* without entering the debate about what Shakespeare intended to keep and what to excise. If, for example, the soliloquy 'How all occasions do inform against me' was intended for excision, then that would make sense in terms of the play's containing only one speech about delayed action. If this cut is made, argues Jones: '*Hamlet* is still a play about procrastination; but now procrastination has been brought into balance and made more justly ponderable within a larger frame.'

Jones's own view, in sum, is that 'the good quarto is a working draft which gets significantly revised in the Folio'. Perhaps more revisions still would bring us a truer *Hamlet* than any to date. Any revision would have to be based upon the idea of a movement towards stability between the two printed editions cited.

Working from the idea of a singular text, it is interesting to see how Jones's discussion of which soliloquy might, with coherence, be excised, is conducted with reference to Bradley and the influence of the novel on Shakespearean criticism. We are familiar with the influence of the psychological novel upon the idea of character in Shakespeare's plays. It would, however, appear that the idea of the authoritative and singular text also carries over from the novel, for this, in the nineteenth century, was refined and professionally edited before achieving its finished and immutable form. Raymond Williams's (1981) discussion about the influence of the editor seeks to persuade us that editors and their publishing houses had such power that they could effectively channel and shape both the form and content of the draft of the novel that the author presented to them. Changes, of an essentially superficial kind, to the text presented by the author would have occurred (as they still do) in the transition between handwriting (or typing) and print. However, power over creative decisions at a deeper level can be understood in terms of the publisher's ideas about what would sell to whom, when and in which form, length or episodic structure. These significant influences of publisher over author would have impressed themselves upon the work in hand well before the final manuscript was received. The reason why we invoke this résumé of Williams's ideas is to suggest that those responsible for the printing and distributing arrangements saw fixity and mass production of the same, but controlled, words as crucial to the enterprise of presenting and selling a fiction. *Hamlet*'s printers, although influential on the text and well aware of what might provoke censorship, were neither as influential at earlier stages of script composition nor as concerned with the ideological dimension in the fixity of the published play.

You might in Shakespeare's time have had to change the words in a play depending upon who was on the throne. Fixity at that time, therefore, might have been against a printing house's self-interest. If, perhaps, we strip away the nineteenth-century varnish in our attempt to recover the *Hamlet* that Shakespeare intended, we find the notion of singularity dissolving somewhat. For all that, we have to be careful where we tread and acknowledge that the lack of an autograph edition of the play does not amount to its being forever fluctuating in form. The would-be producers of a staged *Hamlet* have clearly different readings from which to select in deciding on their script. No doubt parts of what we now assume to be the Shakespeare text were given us by Hemminge and Condell and have become authenticated, as it were, after the event, but we assume that one man wrote the play.

No doubt *Hamlet* was composed in collaboration with others, or at any rate with actors in mind around whose characteristic styles and speech rhythms dialogue was shaped. In part our speculation here is encouraged by the play within the play's conscious attention to aspects of acting, but for all that it seems hard to claim for *Hamlet* that it is a multi-authored work.

What do we conclude from this brief exploration of the idea of singularities as applied to *Hamlet*? It is foolish not to believe that a singular and fully revised edition was intended, and what evidence we have about small additions between the good Quarto and the Folio does not amount to concluding that someone such as a printer added them. However, Jones does convince that what has power as a critical manoeuvre is the study of revisions, of understanding how Shakespeare might work upon a text which is changing in his mind over time, and, presumably, changing by performances within his time. To us there is something of a pre-echo, in this extended editing process, of modern writing conditions. The concept of Shakespeare drafting at his word processor may be the amusing basis for a cartoon, but such a vignette's capacity to indicate continual revision of what Jones calls 'the play's personality' is not absurd at all. Jones's critical position is drawn from a dynamic, that of the movement between two possible versions.

What matters more perhaps than any doubting of the singular author and the variant state of the script is the notion of the *Hamlets* we can inherit, as at any rate notions of films, television productions and radio-broadcast *Hamlets*. Not all of these need to be re-written scripts of the original play that depart deliberately from a respectable scholarly edition, but re-casting any Shakespeare play for a modern medium often requires considerable alteration at the script level as well as a re-casting of the idea of the 'text', which becomes no longer script or theatre performance but something to be seen on screen and/or heard through magnetic recording.

We now have available a sufficient variety of filmed *Hamlets* (47 according to Taylor, 1994) to make questions of script differences well worth studying if we are concerned with the reception of the play within our own sets of cultural concerns. Questions about re-writing and changes of medium are central questions for those of us concerned with the effects of medium upon language, rhetoric and form.

Take, for example, what Taylor (1994) has to say about the Olivier *Hamlet*, filmed in 1948. That film emphasized Hamlet's inner life partly by the device (impossible or at least odd in a theatre) of having the words of the soliloquies as voice-overs and partly by the editing of the original lines to fewer than half their original number. This study of the individual Hamlet composed one possible reading of the play, 'An essay in Hamlet', as Olivier styled it. Such a psychological re-working of the play stood in contrast to a central focus of Kozintsev's film, wherein the outer political dimensions of the play, the governance of Denmark, were given a scope altogether denied in Olivier's.

Different films of *Hamlet* might be no more significant, except for their durability, than different staged performances. They stand both as fulfilments of the script's intentions and as critical interpretations – each one a possibility among a set, but as such they could have great power in an educational context. The same point applies when we consider *Hamlet* in relation to more recently developed media. Already CD-ROMs exist which draw upon comparisons between moments within filmed performances and relate these moments to broader critical enquiries, thus linking performance and critical commentary more immediately than has generally been possible in the past. Such devices cast the audience of learners in a certain analytic role, and it is up to the teacher to turn these analyses into occasions where involvement and thinking together help a growing understanding. We can see how it might be no great difficulty for students to step from watching a scene to acting it out with an interpretive intention in mind; *that* student performance could itself become videoed, thus providing yet another text, ephemeral perhaps, but a point of reference all the same.

What the students would be doing in effect would be adding their text to others, which may well have been created as responses to each other but which all drew from an original script. Criticism becomes textual re-making, and the degrees of collaboration, borrowing and accrued wisdom about what is plausible become explicit, or at least somewhat explicit, in the process. As Sven Birkerts (1994) remarks of the influence of Woody Allen upon an audio-taped version of the novel *The Maltese Falcon*, by Dashiell Hammett: 'The listener gets half-remembered images from the original film and then an overlay of the images that later spoofed those images. Underneath it all, somewhere, is Hammett's text.'

We borrow Birkerts's argument here because it is in precisely these kinds of directions that the technology is leading the *Hamlet* text. The re-writings of *Hamlet* for the stage, by the way, such as *Rosencrantz and Guildenstern Are*

*Dead* and *The Skinhead Hamlet*, show no more reverence towards what Kress categorizes as a 'revered text' than does Woody Allen's *Play It Again Sam* to the original *Casablanca* movie.

Finally, we may want to question the idea of a single text at a deeper level still. What has been said above assumes that the creator(s) of the text(s) are individually or severally 'the onlie begetters' of it. If a text is viewed as a physical artefact then the question of who physically produced it is generally quite easily answered. However, if we ask who creates what the inscription means, then the answer is far less clear. One route leads away from the physical inscriber back to those who influenced that person and his or her mode of writing. But another route leads across from the physical producer to those who read and interpret the inscription, and in so doing create a range of variant texts in the sense that they each set the inscription within a different context and personal history. Indeed, it has been pointed out that each successive reading of a text, even by the same reader, will be a different reading; the previous experience of reading will inevitably affect the next reading. This will be all the more the case if time elapses between readings, since other life experiences of the reader will affect the reading too. One of the leading proponents of this role of the reader as a co-creator of the text has been Louise Rosenblatt, who began to explore this idea as early as the 1930s in *Literature as Exploration* (Rosenblatt, 1938). More recently in *The Reader, The Text, The Poem* (1978), she argues that the literary work ('the poem') in some sense inhabits the space between what is provided by the author ('the text') and what is brought to it by the reader. Now, with the new technologies, the reader can make his or her insights into the text a physical reality as the text is 'played with' or physically transformed on the screen. We return to this and what it might look like in the dynamic classroom of the potentially near future in the last chapter.

Such work on the collaboration with the author by the reader to make meanings takes on an added dimension when groups of readers are involved. The implications of this for the teaching of poetry in the conventional classroom have been well explored in Dias and Hayhoe (1988) but, as we shall see below, with the virtual classroom, members of the group discussing *Hamlet* do not have to be physically present in one space but can operate as groups spread over distance and even time, an electronic equivalent to an extended telephone conference but one achieved much more easily and at a fraction of the cost.

What this extended consideration of the case of *Hamlet* shows is that to think in terms of a single written or printed text by a single author is, if not wrong, at least unduly restrictive. To view it as simply a written or spoken text is likewise too limited, for the performances of the written text are themselves texts, though ones which are spoken and acted. Similarly, a filmed *Hamlet* is also a text, but a multimedia one. Today, therefore, we already have many ways of thinking about the relationship between author, text and medium, and of realizing these relationships in practice, quite independently of any changes that the introduction of new technologies may bring. But what effect will the introduction of these new technologies have upon the terms of this debate, and upon the practicalities of implementing different conceptions of the relationships betwen texts, media and authors? And what are the implications for education of the bringing together of new technologies and the age-old crafts of creating and interpreting texts?

## Technologies: the text maker's tools

To illustrate this we look in turn at some of the text-making tools provided by new technologies. We have chosen to deal with those programs and applications which are commonly used today. While we recognize that technologies change quickly and that the classifications we have used will date, the issues we identify are generic and will therefore continue to be relevant. We focus in particular on the possibilities that are opened up for the creation of single and multiple texts and the ways in which they can enable both individual and collaborative authorship.

### Word processing

Word processing offers a useful starting point for this exploration, for it will already be familiar to most readers. Clearly the task for which desktop word processors (and even more so those built into laptop and palmtop computers) are designed is the creation of single texts by single authors. In this respect they are little more than a well designed typewriter with the addition of some conventional advice on spelling and style. Within these limits they are effective tools, particularly for the production of texts that follow clearly established formulas. Thus most advanced word processing programs contain ready-made templates for writing memos, faxes and even letters and reports, which can be customized by the user to fit particular needs. However, they also contain the beginnings of a more radical form of authorial support, as Tuman (1992) has noted. Allowing the writer to create and store as many sequential versions of a text as may be required, the word processor makes it easier to develop the text while at the same time weakening the impression of fixity and stability that permanent forms of recording reinforce. Yet the same technology, along with laser or inkjet printers, allows the ordinary user to produce something that looks as good as a professionally published document because, in many cases, it actually is as good as far as appearance is concerned. In the case of pupils in schools, this can provide a powerful motivation as their words can look so good on the printed page. On the other hand, this 'quality' may be at a surface level only: it does not necessarily enhance the actual quality of the work produced except in the most superficial way. Thus the text produced is simultaneously experienced by the author as less permanent and thus less significant than a traditionally produced text; at the same time it is experienced as more 'serious' and prestigious. This, in itself, distinguishes word processed texts very firmly from earlier forms of writing.

However, a word processor is manifestly no more physically designed to enable collaborative writing than a car is designed to enable collaborative driving. The word processor, as originally devised, is a tool for writing by one (adult-sized) author only. In this it only follows a long tradition in classrooms and workplaces, where writing technologies nearly always support individual use. The pencil, for instance, is hardly a device designed for team effort, or a notepad something of a size and robustness to make physical sharing of the writing upon it easy. In practice then, group writing in classrooms can disintegrate into one scribe and one dictator, or one writer and one spell-checker, or, worse still, one silent attendant. It is perhaps significant that the one classroom device that does lend itself to shared use, the blackboard (and its successor, the whiteboard) is characteristically reserved for a single user, namely the teacher.

Brine (1991) notes in a Canadian study of primary children that:

> the distance from the screen to the keyboard made it difficult to look back and forth, whereas when writing by hand children looked at the writing instrument and the surface simultaneously. Thus, composing or editing on the screen frequently deteriorated to a preoccupation with the keyboard rather than the task of writing.

Using a computer helper was a solution employed to deal with numerous requests to the teacher for help as children used the computer to write. However, the helper often dominated the computer session, leaving the other student a passive observer. Furthermore, the helper's time was diverted from his or her own work. Even with a helper, the teacher's assistance was often required. Valuable time that might have been used to teach writing was wasted as the teacher became a trouble-shooter for computer problems.

Graves (1983), in his National Institute of Education study, has shown the value of student conferencing in building a community of writers, and there has been much thought given to the ways in which having several pupils grouped around a screen might enable this. But, in practice, group work is often a function of maximizing access to computers and any collaborative work that results takes place by accident rather than as part of a planned pedagogy (Eraut and Hoyles, 1989). This finding was borne out during classroom observation, where pupils grouped together (that is, physically sitting around a single table) were often observed to be undertaking parallel tasks rather than collaborative work. As Scrimshaw (1993) observes: 'simply putting learners together in front of a computer will not ensure peer facilitation of their learning.'

If, therefore, we want to generate deliberate collaborative work both in writing and in the talking on which the writing will be based, we need to plan and teach in such a way as to achieve this end. The technology will not, in itself, change or determine the culture of the classroom.

Yet despite the problems they have to overcome, teachers very often (and rightly) do their best to overcome the difficulties and encourage collaborative word processing, using their skills and support to make up for the limitations of the equipment itself, which is now being used for a pedagogic purpose very different from that for which is was originally designed. What is needed is not to drop the idea of collaborative writing but to find ways of encouraging it.

*Desktop publishing*

Suppose, however, that we accept that the word processor is best used by single authors composing a single text. Can it be extended in other ways that would widen its applicability to writing of different kinds? It can be, and has been, so extended with the development of the desktop publishing package.

In many cultures the distinctions between art forms are relatively alien. As technologies have developed, so the art forms have diverged: it takes an expert to experiment so as to exploit fully the potential of tempera, water colours and oils, as it does the subtleties of timpani, vibraphone and gamelan, or of verse-form, assonance and the iambic pentameter.

Ironically, as the arts have further evolved, the boundaries between art forms have eroded; indeed, many well established art forms, such as opera and drama, have, as we saw in the previous chapter, always involved a combination of media, but this move towards integration has greatly increased in the past hundred years. In the area of printed texts, the increasing interest in picture books where the images and words create a whole, rather than the pictures merely illustrate the words, however beautifully, is an example of this generic drift.

In classrooms the articulation of differing and combining perspectives gives rise to understandings about the creation and readings of texts. By placing two or more parallel genres in juxtaposition, Henry James's *The Turn of the Screw*, for example, as story, play, opera and film, students can perceive some of the decisions of each creator and make judgements about the effectiveness of the messaging in each genre.

In schools where students have worked with artists using a variety of media, their self-esteem, confidence and attitudes to learning have been transformed. They come to realize that their own preferred style of learning is not outlandish and that it is only one on a continuum of styles of learning and response. They can then more comfortably accept the dominant mode often imposed upon them by schooling.

This movement is exemplified in the case of writing by the evolution of the word processor into the desktop publishing package. Such packages now allow multi-columned pages, headlining and the inclusion of pictures and graphs, with an increased requirement for skill and imagination on the part of the user, together with a consequent need for publication skills in the areas of design and layout. Users will, for example, have to come to think in terms of integrating a 'designed' written text within the page, and the ways in which a variety of typefaces may be combined with artwork so as to communicate effectively in intellectually and aesthetically satisfying ways.

However, such packages as currently exist are still in many ways quite conventional; often assuming, for example, standard width columns and rectangular slots for pictures that do not make the creation of, say, a graphic novel or story very easy. Nevertheless, they open up the potential for the creation of a new range of texts by pupils.

*Using electronic mail*

There is nothing new about the idea of several writers producing a number of written texts that are in some way related to each other: sequences of articles in learned journals, 'part' magazines and, in particular, exchanges of letters are all well known examples. Personal correspondence is a form of writing that shares some features with conversation, in that it is directed to a known audience. There is now an electronic analogue to this traditional genre in the form of e-mail. Interestingly, this is evolving in ways that blur the distinction between writing and speaking even further.

The kind of e-mail system which staff in academic institutions are able to use simply adds another network to an already given set of lines of communication across an organization, and it is hard to see how such a web could be exactly reproduced inside a school. However, between groups and individuals within clusters of schools, the possibilities for e-mail are waiting to be fully developed. The kinds of stories already told are encouraging; they support the idea of pupils talking to one another about aspects of culture and language across large geographical distances (totally invisible on e-mail) and, for all that the writers know, large social distances too. One of the characteristics of e-mail is its anonymity: you, as reader, know nothing about the age, gender, race or status of your correspondent until this is deliberately revealed to you as an act of conscious choice. Examples of collaborative curriculum projects using distance communication have been recorded in Keep (1991), and work is currently taking place in which pupils from different countries are engaging together in collaborative writing projects. This 'collaboration at a distance' is so far producing more practical results in terms of collaboration than work in conventional classrooms, since it is of its very nature innovative.

E-mail has been observed as having a stylistic quality more like written speech than like conventional writing, something which its immediacy and speed allow and render seemingly proper in the context. It is a characteristic of the medium that the reader is encouraged to reply as soon as the message has been read, leading to both speed and informality in communication. This 'speech-like' quality of the medium is part of its ability to help young writers, but we need to unpack a little more fully the linguistic and psychological elements involved.

After the advent of the tape recorder, but before the computer, we were certain that writing was not like speech; you do not have to use the sentence, as traditionally conceived, as the basic semantic unit of speech in the same way as you do in writing. Writing enables the containment and embedding of more subordinate clauses than does speech, and it allows various sentence types which are perfectly proper yet which, if spoken, would sound wrong in one way or another. E-mail users quickly discover that the medium has more in common with the telephone call than with the letter, or, possibly more accurately, that to send an e-mail message is more like leaving a message on an answering machine, but with adequate time to compose it. The communicative form which is chosen shapes the way in which the writers come to understand what they are doing, which, in turn, has an effect upon the way they see themselves. This affects the style and the generic customs of the medium.

Those in the habit of e-mailing instead of telephoning people, or instead of writing them memos, write a great deal. They become habitual writers, usually in the form of short notes and messages, requests, greetings, bits of information, answers to questions, questions to which they seek answers – a kind of written chatter, mere scribbling, perhaps. But in these fragmentary bits of maintenance literacy they nevertheless exercise their writing skills and sustain their writerly identity as one of a group. This was a privilege always available to leisured letter writers, but it is now a form of communication that is available to many. They have to take care each time they write of the usual self-representation that any act of writing entails, but it is casual and relaxed in the e-mail world and writers within it do not have to worry too much about a lower case 'i' occasionally, or a misspelling or two.

However, they do have to learn that a new set of conventions is developing for e-mail, often known as 'netiquette', which it is important to understand if one is to avoid giving offence; for example, the fact that the use of block capitals is in e-mail terms the equivalent of shouting at someone.

Everyone knows that one-to-one notes are likely to be done in a hurry without the aid of a spell-checker. However, e-mail allows you to write to lots of people at once and so, for the more general broadcasts, spelling counts far more. Discovering as an apprentice writer with access to an on-line system what the conventions are around here, wherever 'here' may be, is all part of discovering how writing functions as a social as well as purely intellectual or 'art' activity. E-mail is a form of collaboration: messages can be added to, replied to, forwarded and copied to others with mechanical ease; accumulative writing appears to have been an assumption of those who constructed the systems; a veritable 'community of writers' comes about in fact.

The word 'discovering' above does not mean that one consequence for the teaching of literacy is handing over instruction to 'discovery methods' and then doing nothing more, as teacher, than arranging access to the networks. In our view those who have for some time been advocating explicit teaching about genres would seem to have much to contribute. Initiates in e-mail would be helped by looking at a whole range of typical messages and being shown how to understand what the key stylistic and social moves are. The determinants on a grid might be: old form/new form; private/public; formal/informal; or chatter/discourse. The point is that the young writers will, in becoming habitual e-mailers, have engaged in a collaborative series of dialogues which, in their construction, develop increased skill at, and understanding of, the reading/writing interrelationship, entry to a highly verbal context, putting conscious frames around some pieces of writing (the 'attachments') but leaving others open, return or deletion, headlining and summarizing for the 'subject' entry and, in shifting text, editing as a craft skill rather than just as an elite occupation.

In this new medium, then, a new vocabulary and syntax are developing, yet these changes in language may mask more significant continuities in underlying social attitudes. How one secondary school student, Tara Mustapha, sees this is shown in the short story in Figure 2.1.

*Computer conferencing*

Computer conferencing is a variant upon e-mailing in which each member of a predefined group is able simultaneously to send electronic messages to all the others. As with e-mail, these messages are then stored for the recipients, who find them waiting for them when they next switch on their computer. Individuals reply if and when they wish rather than as in a face-to-face group discussion. From this interaction a collaboratively written text evolves over a period of days or weeks and is stored on each participant's computer, this text comprising all the messages sent and received in time order: in effect, a 'transcript' of the discussion.

Such conferences can be highly formalized, with prespecified tasks and strict time limits requiring, for example, all those wishing to contribute to do so within a week of the conference being first set up, and irrelevant contributions being excised by the moderator or chair of the conference. Other conferences may be very informal and long-running, serving a more social purpose. They also vary in size, from those with a few participants to those with hundreds, many of whom may read but not wish to contribute. Larger conferences of this kind are also usually sub-divided into sub-conferences, each covering a particular interest or aspect of the conference topic.

It is possible for classes of pupils in different locations to work together on the same text, sharing their insights through computer conferencing. For example, at the present time, in one development known to us, there are pupils in schools in Australia, Canada and England, simultaneously working on the same short stories set in each of the three countries and building up their understanding of the stories by interrogating their peers about the background cultures involved.

What we have here is yet another new and distinctive form of communication. Whereas e-mail can be seen as growing out of the idea of exchanging

**Figure 2.1**

---

*Race*

She sat herself down in front of the computer and turned the screen on. It was a beautiful day outside but she couldn't be bothered with nature at the moment because she had an appointment with someone on CompuServe. The big 12 × 16 inch, 256 Super VGA screen began to show the colour of her 'Windows '95' display. She grabbed the two button grey mouse and moved the pointer on the START button, selected the CompuServe icon and the screen changed to the CompuServe display. She quickly moved the pointer up to the tool bar and selected the 'Connect' icon. The modem started dialling when she stepped into the kitchen and grabbed a glass of 'Diet Coke'.

The office, where all the electronic equipment was, was conveniently placed connecting to the kitchen so she could grab a snack or drink without having to really leave the computer. As she sat back down she could hear the almost silent hum coming from the Central Processing Unit. When the computer entered CompuServe, a female voice came from the speakers and said 'You have new mail waiting.' CompuServe was a program that connected her to the rest of the world. Through the modem she could find out information about things in a click of a button and she also had E-mail penpals from Australia, Germany, Spain, Africa, Canada, England and the States. She often went on CompuServe to talk to people on the CB band where she met new people every day, some of them male, female, nice, rude, perverts, kids, adults of all different origin. That's where she was going today.

When she entered she went straight to channel 7–The Teen Channel. As soon as she entered, the tracking box showed her handle;

*RAGE* has entered

|  |  |
|---|---|
| *RAGE* | HEY Y'ALL!?! |
| ALEX | DON'T call me THAT! |
| Ex-LAX | :) :( :) :( :) :) |
| CONVICT | whussup RAGE? |
| Sooda | CUL8R |
| POP | Hey RAGE! |
| Gecko | whaT'S UP RAGE? |
| ROMEO | >--------->> a rose 4 rage |
| *RAGE* | Y'us tis fine. the sky is up |
| and | t'y'all howz ya doin'? |
| ALEX | Myra this CPU just called me |
| an | Asshole. |
| myra | BRB |
| ** FURY HAS LEFT THE TEEN CHANNEL* | |
| ROMEO | *{:-{)>----- Santa!! |
| *RAGE* | AGE/Sex/LO/CHEK |
| BLAH | I'M HERE U DWEEBS!! |
| ROMEO | <<-------17/M/DETROIT |
| BLAH | 14/M/LAS VegAS |
| ALEX | 13/f/Orlando |

| aNT | 15/M/ANCHoragE |
|-----|----------------|
| CONVICT | 16/F/ALCATRAZ!!! |
| GECKO | rofl . . . 18/f/MONTREAL |
| Ex-lax | 14/m/Germany |
| Myra | 16 female AUSSIE!! |
| *RAGE* | LONDON FEMALE |

It didn't matter that she hadn't ever met anyone there although some of them were regulars like her. Everyone was friends or enemies. In her mind she could picture what people looked like by what they said, but a lot of the people lied.

| Darknight | who cares where you are from or how old you are! I sure as hell don't! |
|-----------|--------|
| Ex-lax | DID WE ASK YOU? |
| CONVICT | Hello 2 u 2 Darknight <sarc> |
| Darknight | 0000H I'm sorry did I hurt your feelings? haha |
| *RAGE* | why don't you go and hang out with your little clique, your darkriders? WE HAVE BETTER THINGS TO DO THAN RGUE WIT U. |

This conversation evolved into one that consisted of what her mother would call 'vulgar language' in each line. This argument was mainly between Darknight and herself but *RAGE* was like a different ego to her, to Surai. Surai wasn't one to use 'vulgar language'; *RAGE* was. Surai wasn't 16; *RAGE* was. Her argument was interrupted when the sound of a bell rang through the computers' speakers. A girl called Lisa had chosen to speak with *RAGE* in a private conversation box. *RAGE* closed the teen channel conversation and replied to Lisa.

Hi What's up?
Hi! Not much and u?
Oh nothing. I'm just hanging around.
I'm pretty new here. I've only been on for about A WEEK
oH YEAH! UM w.y.r.n.?
What's W.Y.R.N.?
Oh sorry! it's What's Your Real Name?
Oh! It's Lisa W.Y.R.N.?
Mine's Surai. I live in London.

Over an hour of talking to each other they found they had a lot in common.

So what's London like?
Oh, it's pretty interesting, there is lots of traffic, it rains a lot, it's cold and very grey. What's Oregon like?
It's . . . Green.
That all?
Yup :)

More time passed and more stories were shared.

WhAT DO U think of that Brit. band trying 2 get in 2 the States?
What do u mean. Take That? I think they r crap!
Yup, SAME HERE!

> I like Swing. R&B and Rap
> YEAH sAme here, NotoriousnB.I.G., IMMATURE, JANET, Dr. DRE,SNoop, etc.
> YUP!!!

Even personal stories were shared.

> So what's your mom like?
> She seems a lot like yours, nice, strict, has no idea about my life
>     works hard, works late, you get the picture!
> Yeah I' in the same boat.

A month of speaking to each other daily, they decided to send each other photos through the E-Mail. Lisa had blonde hair, green eyes and a few freckles. She had thin lips and straight white teeth after going through a few years of braces.
    Surai had brown eyes and hair and full pouty lips and braces.
    When Surai returned to the CB band she found Lisa.

> Hi! How are you? I got your picture.
> I
> YOU DIDN'T TELL ME YOU WERE BLACK.

Stunned and confused Surai replied.

> You never asked!
> LOOK JUST LEAVE ME ALONE. I DON'T TALK TO DUMB NIGGERS.
> Can't you see, we have so much in common, does skin colour really matter?
> YES IT DOES
> After this I don't want 2 talk 2 u neway, u r shallow and closed minded.
> Girl, colour is only skin deep. Go back to the hole that u came from.

---

letters, conferencing is modelled more on conversational exchanges within a group, and, to some extent, it mirrors the internal variety of such exchanges. On the other hand, it is still a written form, and one of the contradictions within it (as with e-mail) is the tension between the demands and conventions of written and spoken language.

On this tension, Brent Robinson (1993) notes that:

> [There is a difference] between the expectations of teachers about good language use and that language use that the medium encourages. Electronic communication certainly seem to employ different standards of what is acceptable written language use. The style of much electronic linguistic exchange is informal, lying somewhere between the very different stylistic conventions and structure of speech and writing. This is likely to have implications wherever electronic communications are used in the curriculum. In time, as electronic communications become more widely used, there may need to be a revision of accepted norms of what constitutes good style in relation to expression in this medium, or even in relation to writing generally. In the meantime, there could be a positive spin-off if attention to the idiosyncratic style of electronic communication encourages greater language awareness.

Such conferences, like e-mail, are commonly used for factual or social exchanges, but there is no reason why they cannot be used for role playing instead. Indeed there are a number of examples of such uses. In one of life's odder coincidences, both Brent Robinson (1993) and Bernadette Robinson (1993) have useful discussions of this topic, and of the educational role of e-mail and conferencing more generally. However, there are also kinds of software specifically designed to provide collaborative role playing opportunities, and it is to these that we turn next.

## Playing in multi user domains

Multi user domains (or MUDs as they are generally known) became widely available in the early 1990s, though they derived from other genres well established in the early days of home and school computing, the text-only adventure games for example, which, in their turn, derive from fantasy games of the Dungeons and Dragons variety. They are of interest to the English teacher because they combine elements of the home computer game and of e-mail, both of which are culturally significant forms for teenagers today. Mary Fowler (1994) has demonstrated the benefits of enabling young people to make connections between schooled literacies and those associated, for example, with computer games; it seems to us that such approaches will generally become more common and encompass a growing range of texts.

MUDs, in their present form, involve a kind of real-time role play in a virtual world, within which the user can establish a fictional character and then interact with the others present and also with the 'physical' world of the simulation, moving from place to place and modifying the environment – for instance, by moving objects or building something – within the limits set by the rules of the microworld. Characters meet others present in that location at the same time, and they may talk to and interact with them by typing in comments or actions at the keyboard. The results of each user's inputs are displayed for all the others to see as they occur. As Sherry Turkle (1996) describes it:

> MUDs are a new kind of virtual parlor game and a new form of community. In addition, text-based MUDs are a new form of collaborative written literature. MUD players are MUD authors, the creators as well as the consumers of media content. In this, participating in a MUD has much in common with script writing, performance art, street theater, improvisation theater or even comedia dell'arte. But MUDs are something else as well.
>
> As players participate, they become authors not only of text but of themselves, constructing new selves through social interaction. One player says, 'You are the character and you are not the character, at the same time.' Another says, 'You are who you pretend to be.' MUDs provide worlds for anonymous social interaction in which one can play a role as close to or as far away from one's 'real self' as one choses . . .
>
> On MUDs, one's body is represented by one's own textual description, so the obese can be slender, the beautiful plain, the 'nerdy' sophisticated . . . The

anonymity of MUDs – one is known only by one's character or characters – gives people the chance to express multiple and often unexplored aspects of the self, to play with their identity and to try out new ones.

Just as e-mail creates a new communications genre, somewhere between conversation and letter writing, so MUDs represent a new kind of literary genre, for which conventions are only now beginning to evolve. Already, the form is beginning to develop internal variants. In particular, although most, as Turkle's description indicates, are text-only, some MUDs are beginning to appear with graphics. The Japanese computer company Fujitsu, for example, runs a MUD involving thousands of players, in which those taking part can choose their characters to be shown on the screen with a physique and head chosen from a range supplied (animal heads included). The characters appear on screen against a background representing the street or building in which the player has chosen to set them; they can move to other locations within the virtual town that Fujitsu have provided, the screen characters duly walking rather jerkily off to their new position on command. How life within this fictional community develops is up to the players – on one occasion, for example, two of the characters decided to get married, sent out invitations to other characters and were married at a service attended by several hundred of their virtual neighbours. The confusion that this represents between 'virtual reality' and 'the real world' is very complex and we may wonder whether some of the words in the previous sentence should have been put inside quotation marks, and if so, which and why.

## CD-ROMs

CD-ROMs are devices for storing information that operate on the same basic principles as the now-common audio CD. They differ from audio CDs in that they are multimedia; they can therefore be used to store and play back a much wider variety of information: text, diagrams, photographs, animations and computer programs can all be included as well as sound.

CD-ROMs store far more material than floppy disks. This allows the designer to include around a quarter of a million pages of text on each disk, or to include items such as good quality sound and animations (including short video clips) that take up so much space that only a CD-ROM can hold enough of them to provide an effective presentation. Consequently CD-ROM titles range from word-only designs, through multimedia encyclopaedias (where the text is leavened with many pictures and some sound and video clips) to CD-ROMs whose most obvious characteristic is a great deal of animation and sound, such as the very popular talking animated story books produced for younger children.

CD-ROMs can only be read by the user rather than directly modified, although their best usage in classrooms can occur when material is copied off them for later manipulation. They are multi-authored, at least to the same extent that a film or theatrical production is, as they need the combination of the skills of designers, illustrators, programmers and writers to produce the final product.

They can take different forms, allowing, for example, a large corpus of works by a single author or a set of authors with some shared characteristics to be presented to learners as an entity. If the corpus is provided with good facilities for conducting a search, the whole set of texts can be investigated for common features that enable the learner to identify ways in which texts from within the corpus are related by patterns of similarities and differences. Similarly, CD-ROMs which are multimedia encyclopaedias can be searched for background information on writers and their social and literary context.

CD-ROM technology has brought important advances upon the single conventional printed text, for one of its most important characteristics is the capacity to construct a single text from many linked texts, known as a hypertext. Historically, one evolution has been towards the idea of a set of linked texts by a sole author, each requiring a knowledge of the others to gain its full significance. Traditional examples of such explicitly interrelated texts by a single author include the serially published novels of the nineteenth century, the modern novel sequence (of which there are many, Snow and Raven as well as Powell, for example), together with short stories built around the same central characters and locations, as in Hemingway's *The End of Something*.

The hypertext, however, revolutionizes the possibilities here. A hypertext has been defined by Bolter (1991) as consisting:

> of topics and their connections, where again the topics may be paragraphs, sentences, individual words, or indeed digitized graphics. A hypertext is like a printed book that the author has attacked with a pair of scissors and cut into convenient verbal sizes. The difference is that the hypertext does not simply dissolve into a disordered bundle of slips, as the printed book must. For the author also defines a scheme of electronic connections to indicate relationships among the slips. In fashioning a hypertext, a writer might begin with a passage of continuous prose and then add notes or glosses on important words in the passage . . . the glosses themselves could contain glosses, leading the reader to further texts. A hypertextual network can extend indefinitely, as a printed text cannot.

It is thus a set of short texts, in the form of words or images displayed on the computer screen, linked together by 'buttons' or 'hotspots' on the screen. When the cursor is placed over a button and activated the user is taken to the appropriate linked text, which is then in its turn displayed on the screen; each such screen contains a main text and usually several buttons, linking the reader to a different text to be read next. As with printed texts, there can be links from individual terms to passages, as in an index or chapter headings, or cross-links from one passage to another, or indeed to a completely different text, and, frequently, to a different location where language exists in a different context but without necessarily any cues or clues that this is the case. Learning to navigate hypertext is thus quite complex, and requires a quite different set of reading skills from those with which we are familiar from more conventional texts.

What we have here is a device that, even if we exclude links out to visibly different texts, makes the notion of a single, clearly delimited text ambiguous, as we can view a hypertext either as a single complex entity or as the whole set of different possible texts that various readers might experience as they work through it, the text they actually read depending upon their choice of route.

Hypertexts can be used for factual material, but they can also be used for fiction. What this creates is a quite new conception of a fictional text, in which the author willingly shares control with the reader over what story will be read by providing a choice of links that allow elements to be read in different orders, or even in some cases be by-passed altogether. This is quite unlike the conventional situation, in which the author attempts to maintain strict control over the sequence of reading through methods of directing attention forward and back through the text that are often left implicit, and which rely upon the general conventions of reading a printed book, such as the expectation that the reader reads the text in the order in which it is presented.

An example of the fictional hypertext that has been especially warmly welcomed by primary teachers in the United Kingdom (see Wegerif *et al.*, 1996) is the CD-ROM based interactive book. Phil Moore (1994) observes:

> Adults have grown up using books in which illustrations often provide exemplifications of the words which accompany them. Children, however, are increasingly using and being read books where the relationship between the words and the images is complex. In books for children, the images may directly contradict the words. For example in John Burningham's 'Time to get out of the bath, Shirley' the child reader knows and recognises that the pictures depict Shirley's daydreams while the words convey her mother's reality. This tension between the various levels of text can be explored by the writer in different ways with integrated media. In the CD-ROM, 'Grandma and me' the picture on each 'page' is animated to echo the narrative which appears in words on the screen. Once the narrative is finished, users can click the pointer on different parts of the picture and cause things to happen that were not represented in the narrative – a fish, when clicked on, will kiss the child character, for example. The effects of this are very different from the Burningham book. For example, the 'flights of fancy' which children create for themselves when looking at pictures in books are replaced with actions predetermined by the writers, which are the same with each reading . . . [Nevertheless] . . . this example does demonstrate vividly that writers now have tools to enable users to explore texts in a variety of new ways.

Some packages exist that combine the features of desktop publishing packages and hypertext authoring tools so as to allow pupils to create their own multimedia texts in the classroom. These can be transferred at a later stage to CD-ROMs, which are used as a storage medium. Such packages can also be used collaboratively. What this involves, and why it might be worth English teachers using it, is indicated by Harry McMahon and Bill O'Neill (1993) in their account of a cross-age range research project they conducted in Northern Ireland:

> Children's stories, and it is storying that they do very well, are frequently scattered with the seeds of powerful imaginative ideas. One of the challenges for the teacher is to create frameworks which allow children to continue to sow these imaginative seeds but which also nurture their growth and development and their manifestation in literary form. Central to our thinking was that these supportive frameworks would be constructed by teacher and pupils working collaboratively. The computer might be bought to bear or used as a tool but it was the quality of the interaction that would ensure quality learning.
>
> It appeared to us when we first contemplated taking digitised multimedia into classrooms, that Hypercard provided the central platform of a multimedia environment which would allow this interaction to take place and at the same time challenge learners to seek new and powerful means of expression. The multimedia environment consisted of a Macintosh computer with the Hypercard software and, in addition, a MacRecorder and a scanner. The MacRecorder is a very easy but powerful sound digitiser that allows the learner to incorporate any sound from any source into their work. A scanner will digitise any photograph or drawing and thus allow these to be incorporated directly into children's work. The magic comes about because children are operating with digitised sound, digitised graphics and digitised text; in that form the sound, graphics and text all become fully manipulable, they can be cut and pasted, twisted, turned, separated and linked in any number of ways. Thus in the Hypercard environment, for the first time ever, teachers could allow children's preferred medium to become central, allowing them, for example, to first tell their stories through drawing or music and only then elaborate them with text. Through this integration of and transference between media, children could be caused to reflect on the meaning-making process itself and on the contribution that text, sound/music and photographs/drawings/ graphics can make to the process.

The lack of access to the means of production means that, for a short period of time, CD-ROM authorship is restricted, though this will not always be the case. In any case, other media will supersede the CD-ROM, and are already beginning to do so, so that as a medium it is likely to have a limited role except for very specific purposes.

## The Internet

A few years ago one of us was trying to envisage (Scrimshaw, 1993b) what might represent an educationally optimal new technology. He wrote:

> the integration of a networked hypertext system into a face to face learning culture would have considerable potential, allowing learners to develop their ideas by interacting with others (including teachers) within and across the two contexts. So what might such a system for school use look like?
>
> What would be required is a conferencing system linked to a large database, both presented in a hypertext format. Each learner would need at least some

opportunities to contribute both to the debates carried on the messaging system, and to the evolution of the common database of information. Such a system could also carry assignments and provide programs . . . for learners to use as and when required. Users would also need face to face contact with at least some of the contributing group, and access to teachers, both directly and through the conferencing system. From this nexus of information, activities and discussion with others, learners would be able to evolve their own electronic commonplace book of ideas, examples and evidence, drawing as required from the shared network, and contributing their own ideas back to it as they developed. Yet simply creating such a system would not ensure active, shared learning. The extent to which it became an active learning system would depend also, for example, upon the number of contributors, the extent to which users were really communicating only within relatively closed subgroups, the structure of the hypertext, and the controls over who could make links.

Three years later it is clear that the Internet is showing strong signs of being a medium through which this specification might be more than met, for it also has a multimedia format, which, though technically limited today, will in all likelihood have evolved beyond what we could predict by the time this book is published. In essence, what the Internet provides is a compendium of all the possibilities offered by the media we have already considered. All can be, and most are, available in some form on the Internet, which is basically a network of thousands of mainframe computers, each in turn linked to the personal computers of many individuals. Structurally, therefore, it functions rather like the international telephone and postal systems, providing a channel for communications, via a number of intermediate systems, between any two individuals linked into the network. The latest estimate is that 40 million people may have access to the Internet. This is small by comparison with either the telephone or postal networks, and limited by an estimated 80 per cent of communications at present being made in a single language (English), though a strong reaction is beginning against this domination by the English language and American culture. It is also technically limited in the rates at which information can be transmitted, and in the considerable congestion that is already being experienced by many users, both of which make it often slow in response. Nevertheless, it is still an important development, and more significantly one that offers considerable potential for future expansion and improvement.

The World Wide Web (WWW or Web) is the part of the Internet that most is known about by the general public. It has caught the imagination because it is so attractive and easy to use and because it provides a vehicle for anyone to publish whatever he or she wishes, though this of course is also the reason for much of the adverse publicity which has been directed at the activities of the minority who are using the Web for dubious, and even unlawful, publishing purposes. The Web is essentially a collection of texts, linked together only by the cables and wires that communicate between the millions of computers all over the world on which the texts are stored. It is not classified, like a library, but is searchable, and there are pages with pictures, sounds and words about almost any conceivable subject. The Web has opened up an important avenue for students to author their own multiple texts, or hypertexts, and teachers in a small minority of schools are already exploiting this opportunity.

Many of the issues generated by authoring with the Web are the same as those that arise from working with CD-ROM hypertexts. There is an important difference, however, in the speed with which the texts can change. The connections, or links, that you make as an author of a Web text are to those published by other people, over which you have no control because they do not exist in a permanent or fixed form. For example, if this section were a Web text, we could illustrate a certain point by making a link to pages published by students in a school in South Africa. However, at any point those students might change *their* text in such a way that it ceased to provide the kind of exemplification that *our* text required. Consequently, important new issues about the maintenance of a text have been introduced into the authoring process.

The Internet allows users to e-mail others, to take part in thousands of computer conferences and to access major databases of texts, pictures and sounds around the world. It is also possible to carry out literature searches in major libraries at a distance, to see if they contain what is wanted, and in some areas to subscribe to electronic journals. Much of what is available is provided free by public service institutions such as universities and government departments, but commercial interest is growing rapidly.

It is already possible to order goods by responding electronically to adverts provided at commercial sites on the Internet (including electronic shopping malls), although payment usually has to be arranged off-line, as sending credit card details via the Internet is, at the time of writing, generally considered unwise. With electronic charging, far more commercial services will no doubt become available, competing directly with postal mail order businesses, and indirectly with conventional high street shops. This is particularly likely to make an impact in such areas as news provision through on-line, regularly updated newspapers, sales of software (which can be piped direct into your computer on payment) and service areas such as insurance, credit unions, banking, charity giving, estate agency and share dealing.

Against this vision of the Internet's future can be set the hopes of those who see it as a new electronic continent in which anarcho-syndicalism can flourish, with individuals around the world coming together to cooperate across boundaries of race, gender, nation and class on projects of their own collective choosing.

Probably both possibilities will be realized to an extent, but computer-based developments have never yet met all the expectations of those who favoured them, and in the case of the Internet, there are a number of technical limitations. In attempting to remove these we begin to move from the Internet as we have it now, to the so-called information superhighway, which represents the next stage of development for multimedia, multi-author and multi-text integration.

The term 'information superhighway' is one that has come into popular usage, even though the metaphor employed is somewhat misleading. In essence the term is used as a generic name for the development of the Internet that may come into existence as it becomes possible to use communications technologies to transmit larger amounts of information faster. The basic problem is that copper telephone wire, upon which most Internet communications depend at some stage in their journey, can only carry information at a relatively slow rate. This is perfectly satisfactory for the rapid transmitting of words, reasonable sound and small or relatively low-definition pictures. It can even carry rather jerky animations or digital video pictures, and to some extent the limitations of the transmission network can be compensated for by using more powerful computers and better compression techniques. However, to reach the stage where it is possible to get two-way transmission of instantaneous video to multi-channel television standard (that is, to move from narrowband to broadband transmission) requires different technologies. Various combinations of possibilities are being explored, including fibre optic cable and radio and satellite transmission. In some parts of the world such networks are already in place, with cable TV companies a major source of these. Leaving aside the technicalities, what broadband transmission offers is the possibility of the integrated delivery of video, voice, text and other services (that is, a fully developed form of multimedia), real-time high speed video-conferencing and on-demand video.

The social implications of the development of such networks are considerable, at least within the developed world, and the possibilities are now being explored in many places, including Singapore, Australia and the European Union.

## Conclusion

It will be seen that there are exciting new possibilities being opened up by advances in technology for both reading and writing, and that our conventional idea of texts needs to be widened to include both multiple authored texts and multimedia texts of all kinds. In the following chapter we discuss some of the theoretical implications of this and its effect upon existing models of English teaching, after which, in Chapter 4, we give some specific examples, drawn from current practice, of the ways in which the new technologies are already affecting what teachers do in English lessons. Finally, in Chapter 5, we extrapolate from this what English teaching might be like by the end of the first decade of the twenty-first century.

# 3 A framework for English

At the core of the subject 'English' are words: the words of the language which people need for making and communicating meaning; the words of literature; written words, spoken words. English teachers are all, to a greater or lesser extent, practitioners in what they teach: readers and writers, users of language, writers of words; some might even class themselves 'wordsmiths'. As readers they will also be fluent with images and sound – through children's books, newspapers, television, film and drama. But words are their main business.

Media studies, communication studies and drama have traditionally been the places where students have learned about the moving image, about non-verbal sound, about gesture and about the interrelationships of these systems of representation with words. In practice many English teachers teach about some or all of these but largely in discrete curriculum boxes or as units or topics within the English programme of study. Yet across the world, until quite recently, these areas would not have been regarded as essential to the study of English. Clear evidence of this can be seen, for example, in the forms of statutory assessment that currently predominate in England. Despite an increasing number of students who routinely compose texts using computers and who conduct research and entertain themselves using CD-ROM and the Internet, pencil and paper tests are seen by politicians as the gold-standard and are used to assess students' response to written words.

However, practice in classrooms has been evolving, as we show in Chapter 4, and formal curriculum documents have begun to reflect that evolution, albeit a slow one. It was suggested as long ago as 1984 in the HMI publication *Curriculum Matters 1* (DES, 1984) that 'Every encounter with technology is potentially an encounter with language.' This might well sound like a truism today; yet, in practice, there are still many who would need to be convinced. Nevertheless, the range of types of texts with which some teachers are working has broadened to include media and electronic texts, and the language of media studies is being adopted by teachers who ten years ago might not have been familiar with its conceptual basis. In too many English classrooms, however, as we signalled in Chapter 1, a video is regarded as a visual aid, or a substitute for the printed text for the 'less able' pupils, instead of being seen as an object of study in its own right. Nevertheless, things are changing and we are a long way from the days when most teachers of English saw their main task as being that of 'inoculating' their pupils against the malign influences of the 'mass' media. More productive approaches have been presented in books such as those by Masterman (1980, 1985) and Goodwyn (1992).

This is how two teachers discussed the teaching of *Pride and Prejudice* in 1996, just after a major television production of the novel:

> X: In my own teaching with my PGCE students I have found that, for me, media studies has been the unifying force. Can one teach a Year 12 class in November 1995 about *Pride and Prejudice* without taking note of the TV production? Has the novel been changed by the TV adaptation?
>
> Y: Yes, the novel has been changed – I read it with a more delicate, delicious understanding, by being able to visualize the kinds of rooms, streets and gardens in which the drama is played out. It's the difference between reading a play and seeing it staged. If Lizzie and Darcy aren't the castings I would have made, I can change them for myself, but I can't summon up an appropriate drawing room without significant and distracting research.

## Emerging patterns

In New Zealand, visual literacy is a strand in the new curriculum. In the USA the new strand is mediacy, though there there has been a considerable backlash from the more traditional lobby among the English teaching community, who resist the 'watering down' of their subject by the introduction of media studies. In Australia the National Statement on English, which provides the basis for the state English curriculum, is divided into two strands, 'text' and 'language'. The 'text' strand comprises 'literature', 'everyday' ('mundane' in the sense we have already used the word) and 'mass media' texts, with teachers required to select titles from each. 'Mass media' includes print, film and electronic forms. In Victoria, language modes in the curriculum are grouped as 'reading and viewing', 'writing' and 'speaking and listening'. In England and Wales, the curriculum order which came into force in September 1995 dealt explicitly not just with print and words but with screens and texts, and viewing is explicitly included in the National Curriculum document on the teaching of Welsh, even though it appears, rather curiously, as part of the Attainment Target on speaking and listening.

What is the significance of such changes to English teachers now and for the future?

**Figure 3.1**

**English**
media studies
drama

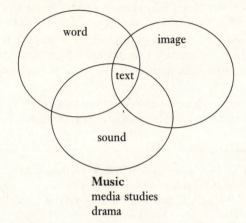

**Art**
media studies
drama

**Music**
media studies
drama

As we argue in Chapters 1 and 2, information technology has changed the landscape in which we are operating. While it is difficult to be clear about how the landscape will continue to develop, it is possible to be sure that there will be no return to that which existed before information technology. There are now new media and new forms for representing meaning, new means for communicating meaning. And as time goes on these will become more surely established, not less. The electronic revolution has generated new areas of study.

Figure 3.1 shows the systems for representing meaning with which the school curriculum has always concerned itself. Traditionally, words have been the preserve of 'English', images of 'art' and non-verbal sound of 'music'. While all subjects deal in some way with the areas of overlap, it is, arguably, only in media studies and drama that there has been a central concern with the interrelationships between the three. Now, with developments in information technology, and the emergence of multimedia texts like CD-ROMs, the central area of Figure 3.1, where words, images and non-verbal sound are all combined, has sprung into sharp relief. And because words are the 'glue' which holds together these new electronic texts, it is to the English curriculum that students will need to turn for guidance on how to read (or use) and write (or compose) such texts.

For English teachers this is less of a departure from tradition than it may appear. Many writers of the past sought to break the bounds of linear print texts and the Ahlbergs have delighted children (and, indeed, adults) with their attempts to stretch the medium of the book to its limits, seen especially in *The Jolly Postman* and *The Jolly Christmas Postman*. Print has never really been the pure form that the current English National Curriculum would appear to suggest. In a curious way we are going back to the future, back to the illuminated manuscript in a new form.

## New models and metaphors for English

It is now the case that, with computer technology, a pupil working in English can make choices about how to work with words, sounds and images, although, as yet, this rarely happens in practice. She could also choose whether to work in the linear ways with which we are now familiar or to create a hypertext of the kind described on pp. 36–7.

With communications technologies, a pupil working in English can also make choices about whom to work with, as an invitation to contribute to a global publication, *Through Our Eyes*, illustrates.

---

To:   UK-SCHOOLS @ mailbase.ac.uk

Dear Writing Teachers Everywhere:

Do your students hate to write descriptive essays? Perhaps having a real purpose and audience would help. Ask your students to choose a place near your community to describe to a global audience. Since our environment shapes our experiences, it becomes an important part of who we are. For example, we live in Laurel, Delaware, USA, not too far from the Atlantic Ocean.

We enjoy swimming, surfing, fishing, and walking on the beach. Where do you live? Describe to us your location. The desert? The prairie? The tundra? The city?

Share your submissions with everyone (even those not participating by sending them out on the KIDPROJ list which acts as a kind of Bulletin Board enabling everyone to enjoy students efforts even if they are not taking part in the project).

We will combine and DTP (Desk Top Publish) them into a hardcopy magazine 'Through Our Eyes' and send each participant a copy.

Replies to:
Regina Royer <rroyer@shore.intercom.net>
24.08.95

---

While such a joint publishing project does not of itself require new thinking about the nature of the English curriculum, it offers a new range of possibilities, for with information technology new forms of collaboration are made possible, as Chapter 4 demonstrates.

A recognition that the new technologies are now part of the landscape that is English was shared by delegates from across the world at a conference in New York in July 1995 of the International Federation for the Teaching of English (IFTE). This was to be seen in the discussions of models and metaphors

**Figure 3.2**

for English, the need to come to a fuller and more complex understanding of what we mean by text and intertextuality, and, above all, the highly visual and dynamic presentation of the work of the groups with which the conference closed (see Figure 3.2).

On return from that conference one of the authors of this book developed Figure 3.3 in order to provide a means for thinking about the differences and similarities between 'old' and 'new' texts. Towards the left-hand end of the continua one would find nineteenth-century novels, war poetry, newspaper articles, Kress's mundane texts. They are stable, linear texts which make references within recognized conventions and are expected by their readers to reach closure.

Towards the right-hand end would sit non-print texts constructed with information technology, such as a page on the World Wide Web or an animated story on CD-ROM. In such texts references can be concrete, with links to the actual texts cited or alluded to; layers of meaning can be physically represented with hypertext and points of closure are unclear.

**Figure 3.3**

| | |
|---|---|
| black and white | colour |
| read only | read/write |
| stable | fluid |
| static | dynamic |
| referential | linked |
| linear | layered |
| closure | non-closure |

English teachers who lack experience with or understanding of the texts which operate towards the right-hand end of these continua will find teaching them a problem and will only learn how to do so by using them in their class-rooms. Indeed, the value of close attention to what children do with these new kinds of texts has been demonstrated by a group of teachers working with CD-ROMs in Redbridge in Essex. For instance, they discovered that it was not until both they and their pupils overcame unrealistic expectations of the new medium that they could exploit it. But over time they also began to realize how they could extend their notions of writing and composition once they understood, for example, that they could edit pictures in the same ways as they could words.

The range and number of possibilities opened up by new technologies might appear to create demands that an English curriculum could not reasonably address. English teachers worldwide will concur that they do not have enough time to do what they have to do. Were new texts to be added to the existing set, something would have to go. Yet teachers would also agree that their business is that of enabling pupils to explore and make meaning and to communicate effectively with others. In order to enable their pupils to become critical readers and writers, they would accept that they should understand about and know how to use all kinds of texts.

While curriculum overload is an important reason for not adding new areas of study as accretions to those which already exist, there is an additional and more compelling one. Bolting new areas on to the old does not work, either for teachers or for pupils. New ideas need to be understood through the making of connections with old ones; new possibilities need to be compared with existing ones in order to establish what are their similarities and differences. If there are, as we maintain, new types of texts, new possibilities in reading and writing, it is essential that pupils learn how these relate to those that are already part of the curriculum.

Making connections emerged as a key principle when the group of people brought together by the National Council for Educational Technology in November 1992 addressed the question of how English should take on the new technologies. It was clear that we needed to re-examine the basis on which the English curriculum is founded; at the 1995 IFTE conference in New York it became evident that this was not a local concern but had become a global necessity.

What emerged from our work proved not to be new, as we had thought it might be. It turned out to be, instead, a bringing together of existing ways of thinking. This was important because it reassured us that what we were doing was not about demolishing existing practice in order to accommodate new texts but about re-formulating and strengthening that which already exists.

One of our commentators writes:

> The shift . . . can only enrich English in my view, if one takes the central concerns of the subject as being to do with texts and identity. The informed and critical reading of texts of all kinds, with attention to linguistic, literary and visual conventions, as well as issues of representation, positioning, ideologies and the like, is clearly going to continue to be central to individuals and to society, as also will be the need to be a maker of texts as writer and reader, viewer, speaker and listener. Fears about 'the end of English as we know it' seem to me to be something of a red herring, not really solved by increasing the emphasis on classic literature or taking a cryogenic approach to linguistic purity. If we can expand our conceptions of both texts and language, the subject becomes not just more 'relevant' to students, but both stronger and more flexible in maintaining its focus on helping students to become critical and active makers and users of text, reflective about themselves and 'the world', about the politics of representation, social justice and identity.
>
> (CB)

## Towards a theory for texts

An approach to defining a literacy curriculum for the twenty-first century through the recommendation of specific texts is clearly not feasible given the expanding corpus, even were it desirable. If pupils were to read examples of every possible type of text in all media, we calculated that they would have to read 8000 texts! Nevertheless, we have to teach pupils to interrogate texts of all kinds, in different media, electronic as well as written; we need to enable pupils to develop their knowledge about texts. Just as we teach knowledge about language in order that pupils become confident language users, so we have to teach knowledge about texts so that they become confident and critical creators and users of texts. In particular, this will mean becoming critical of the new technology as well, understanding that it is not a neutral resource.

This requires a language for talking about texts which derives from a theory about texts – what they are, how they are constructed (with what technologies) and how they are used. The schema in Figure 3.4 shows the kind of framework which we believe could underpin such a theory. It represents a set of concepts which apply both to texts that already exist and to possible new texts or types of texts that may emerge in the future.

The framework is designed to represent a set of categories which apply to all texts (the columns headed 'originator' and so on). Within each of those categories are examples of the range of possibilities that are available to a writer, depending upon the context for the writing (time, place, social, cultural and economic) and upon the available technologies and media, and enabled (or otherwise) by the current gatekeepers. Each of the columns really needs to conclude with a series of etceteras, for we have tried to represent all the possibilities of texts that we can think of at the present time, but there will be others that cannot have been thought of yet and which will need to be represented by the same analytical framework.

We see the framework as being a useful basis for helping young people to answer fundamental questions about any text:

- Who wrote it? Was it one or many people? Do we know who all the authors are?
- What medium was used and how was the text transmitted to its readers?
- Who enabled the text to be published or distributed?
- What is its form?
- What is it for?
- For whom is it intended?

Our expectation is that such an analysis would not replace but would inform the consideration of wider questions about a text, such as: How do its characteristics relate to the context within which it was written? How do those characteristics affect its meaning, effect, quality and significance? What are the effects of using a particular technology? What is the impact or effect of a text on its audience?

Take as an example the process of composition with which we engaged in producing the present text. It is a multi-authored (and edited) text of which the *originator* is a working group. That group consists of various sub-groups: two editor/writers drawn from a group of five core writers; four reader/writers who read the text and contributed their own; six readers who commented on the text in order that the writers could revise it.

The final *representational medium* is print writing, but during the process of construction we have used handwriting and screen text and much of the interaction between authors has taken place through telephone discussions and e-mail messages. In the text you are now reading, images are used sparingly and in a largely secondary relationship to the words; however, we hope

**Figure 3.4**

→ → → → → → → → → → → → → →

I/we represent something | through a medium | via someone's offices | by some means | for my/our reason/s | for someone

| Originator | Representational medium | Gatekeeper | Form | Purpose | Audience |
|---|---|---|---|---|---|
|  | **Single medium** • **Word** live, recorded or computer-generated speech, handwriting, print, screen text, e-mail | **Individual/ institutional** teacher, editor, conference controller, publisher, Internet service provider, Board of Film Censors | **Stable/ plastic** liturgy or memo/e-mail chat, scripted drama/ improvisation, book/word processed file | **Persuade** | **Remote/close** culturally, geographically, socially, linguistically, temporally |
| **Single** | • **Image** photo, painting, computer graphics, sculpture |  |  | **Explore** |  |
| **Multiple** pair, committee, working group, editorial | • **Non-verbal sound** live, recorded, computer-generated song, tune, sound effects | **Visible/ invisible** line manager, Internet provider | **Linear/ non-linear** novel/ encyclopaedia computer conference/ hypertext | **Inform** | **Single/ multiple** individual, class of peers/range of schools |
|  | **Multimedia** dance, theatre performance, film, hypertext, World Wide Web site, TV |  | **Small/large** newspaper article/War and Peace, hypertext card/CD-ROM | **Entertain**  **Express** |  |

by someone | which is represented | through someone's offices | by some means | for our/my reason(s) | I/we read/ view something

← ← ← ← ← ← ← ← ← ← ← ← ← ←

(i.e. I/we read/view for my/our reasons by some means through someone's offices something which is represented by someone.)

that some parts of the text may also appear on the World Wide Web and we expect that those will differ from their print equivalent in both meaning and form.

The *gatekeepers* here were the group appointed as editors, drawn from the original working group, and our publishers, who had to be persuaded not only of the book's potential for sales but also of the format within which we wished to work. We should perhaps also consider as gatekeepers the readers who through their commentaries on the text indicated to us where changes were needed.

The *form* we have chosen is that of the relatively conventional book, though we could have chosen others, such as a series of linked pages on the WWW. The decision reflects our recognition that this is the best means to reach our target *audience*, fellow English teachers on a worldwide scale, at the present time.

Our *purposes* were at least to inform and persuade. We hope also to entertain and influence.

It will be seen that none of the categories can be described as 'pure', and each of them involves the making of choices, some of which continue to be negotiated right up to the time of publication itself. It is significant that although we tried to break some of the boundaries of the printed form, we had to compromise because of our lack of control over the production processes and the economics of book publication. We had planned to use left-hand pages to provide a commentary on the main text – commentary from the authors on their own text and from outside. (The idea for this came to us when we thought of Coleridge's use of marginal commentary in *The Ryme of the Ancient Mariner*.) Instead, the exigencies of conventional print publication have meant that we have had either to incorporate that commentary in the main text or to represent it visually as boxed insertions.

In the future, it seems probable that electronic publishing will dramatically change the traditional relationship between author and publisher. As authors become more accustomed to using desktop publishing programs to compose their texts they will be delivering more complete camera-ready copy; they will be able to write for the page, or the section or chapter, allowing the overall design to shape their use of words and images to represent meaning. That in its turn will affect what can be said.

At the top and the bottom of Figure 3.4 we have used a rubric to show that it is intended to be used for thinking about the reading, or viewing, of a text as well as the writing of it. It may sometimes be helpful for readers to consider the differences in the audiences, purposes and gatekeepers that pertain to the reading of a text from those affecting the writer. Examples of this might be the security videos which are subsequently broadcast for entertainment, or *Great Expectations*, written as a serial for readers of *Household Words* and now studied as an examination text by 16-year-olds.

One of the ways in which students might use our text framework would be to think about how authors achieve their purposes; for example, by making comparisons between the ways in which different novelists work, whether writing in the nineteenth or late twentieth centuries. Students reading Jane Austen would note that for her some of the possibilities represented in our framework would have been markedly different from those available to Salman Rushdie today. Yet Rushdie still chooses to write the print novel. In exploring why Rushdie might have eschewed all the other possibilities open to him, in speculating about how Jane Austen might have exploited the new technologies that are now available, students will have the opportunity to learn not only that writers make choices but also that what they write and how it is read will be affected by both the choices they have made and the society and culture in which they live. Additionally, they will have a framework for making connections between the old and the new; to see, for example, the similarities between the novels of Dickens and the television soaps of today, as well as the differences.

A contributing reader comments:

> Much work in English over the past few years has been dominated by the teacher's concerns about when to use the 'film of . . .' or the 'video of . . .' to accompany work on a text. There is a constant sense of anxiety that the children will confuse the versions and then 'get it wrong in the exam'. We are not dismissing this problem; teachers are simply forced into this concern by the residual elitist view about books. For example, it is still impossible to imagine an English exam question that asked in what way Dickens's novels might be compared to soap operas. The irony is not that the pupils do not know about soap operas (though there is no reason simplistically to presume that 16 to 18-year-olds are interested in them), but they would not know enough about the production and reception of the Dickens's texts to answer in any knowledgeable way.
>
> It would seem essential that at some stage in secondary schooling all pupils should examine the multiple versions of a particular text in order to grasp its significance and what these versions signify. This is not a common practice in media studies. It is only likely to happen in English. Dickens, for example, is 'dramatized' in all kinds of ways, although rarely these days as a feature film; this is almost certainly a matter of fashion, however. At the time of writing Jane Austen is the cinematic and televisual focus of the 1990s. It seems important, as an example, for pupils to recognize what the 'Austen' industry is all about. It is certainly producing some extremely popular and enjoyable new texts. The simplest irony of this industry is that Jane Austen will be read more widely over the next few years than she has been for the previous fifty. Surely pupils should have a chance to think about this cultural phenomenon. There are many interesting questions for English to raise for pupils to investigate about the interest in Jane Austen's work. Equally, they should understand that one episode of *Coronation Street* in the United Kingdom will be watched by far more people than will ever see *Pride and Prejudice*. Who is it that wants them not to understand what is signified by such differences?
>
> This latter point is where English must absorb one of the most significant developments of media studies, the fundamental questioning that it demands of

everyone: pupils, students and teachers. It is inclusive of all kinds of texts and it seeks to give us a way of focusing on texts in powerful ways. It always asks the question that English frequently ignores: how did this text come to be produced? This question immediately raises many others about how texts come to be made and by whom, and then how they come to be reproduced. We feel that this kind of questioning opens up texts to put pupils in a powerful position: they too can produce and reproduce texts from the culture and introduce their own, 'new' texts.

(AG)

Another of our readers gives us this example of how the connections between texts can be productively explored in the classroom:

I teach my preservice English teachers Tennyson's *The Lady of Shalott* as a point of reference for Australian author Jessica Anderson's novel *Tirra Lirra by the River*. Anderson's novel, commonly set at year 12 (A level), is the reflection of an old woman at the end of her life, with specific reference back to the poem and the image of Lancelot recurring throughout. This image 'haunts' much of her journeying, and is eventually linked back to childhood and the death of her father. I use the poem, together with Waterhouse's painting, to introduce both the Arthurian legends and the Victorian uses of them. This lets us into intertextuality, and such matters as conceptions of the relations between life and art, constructions of women, female sexuality, metaphors of the journey, tapestry and so on.

(CB)

## Towards a wider curriculum

If one of the purposes of the reading/writing curriculum is to develop knowledge about texts and confidence with them, the question remains about what those texts should be. It seems to us that *range* will be essential. Within each of the categories represented in the text framework, students will need to work with a variety of different types of text in order to appreciate the full spectrum of the total range of possibilities that exists. It is clearly the case that the curriculum should provide for specific reading and writing experiences. Therefore, all children should be enabled to work collaboratively, as well as individually, and to read and write for different purposes. They will need opportunities to learn about the constraints within which writers work – economic, historical, cultural, linguistic. Through the reading curriculum they will need to learn about the significance of writers' choices. Through the writing curriculum they should exercise a range of those choices. Through the choice of texts, and knowledge about why they were chosen, they should learn about the cultural significance of specific texts. And through an entitlement to use and understand the use of all text-making technologies they will be able to learn about the effect these have on both the processes and products of writing and reading.

In practice, it seems likely that reading and writing curricula will become even more closely linked than they are today. It is significant that even as late as 1971, one of the leading theorists in English teaching at that time, Andrew Wilkinson, in *The Foundations of Language* could talk of writing and talking as *productive* modes of language and reading and listening as *receptive* modes. By now, even the National Curriculum has come to recognize the reciprocal nature of oracy, that speaking and listening are two sides of a single coin. Much work was done to this end by the National Oracy Project in the early 1990s (see, for example, the papers collected in Norman, 1992). It is still not so widely recognized that this is the case with the literacy element of the curriculum, where reading and writing are still separated as distinct attainment targets, although in the 1960s and beyond there has been much interest in the notion of reader response to literature, so that the reader becomes a co-creator of the text with the writer (see Chapter 2, p. 24). This is probably because of the dominance of writing in many English classrooms. In those schools where there is setting for English, the sets are usually determined by a pupil's ability to write; being 'good at English' becomes synonymous with being 'good at writing' (which does not even necessarily mean being 'a good writer', it should be noted). Yet, as the diagram below tries to show, the relationship between reading and writing is both reciprocal and highly complex (this diagram is a representation by one of the writers of discussion in the models and metaphors group at the 1995 IFTE Conference):

Writing    as    Composition    as    Transformation

   as                     as                          as

Reading    as    Reflection    as    Refraction

When we are working with technologies which enable us to combine words, images and sound and to change the texts that others have produced, reading has the potential to become writing, for it is possible to change ('transform') the texts we read, composing new texts from the old. There is the capacity to make reflection on reading concrete and explicit by adding to or changing an existing text. And as a way of reflecting on text, exploring and experimenting with it in a new medium can offer insights into and shifts of meaning that can well be characterized as refraction.

---

In this example, Michael was asked to demonstrate how it was possible to work with a page from a CD-ROM text in order to make it say something different. He chose a piece about ball and socket joints (Figure 3.5) and turned it into a representation of something he had learned earlier that week about hip replacements (Figure 3.6). It was a draft which fulfilled his purpose (or rather, his mother's) to create a text which demonstrated how you can use technology. But because there was no real audience he did not proceed to produce a perfect copy. He could have gone further by making the font size smaller so that his words fitted the frame created by the originator; he would thereby have produced a final copy that was comparable with the original

**Figure 3.5**

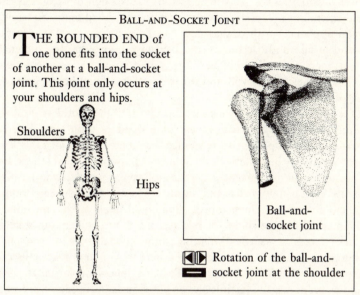

[c] 1994 Dorling Kindersley Multimedia

**Figure 3.6**

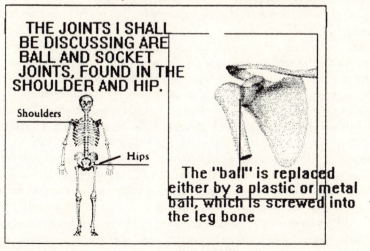

Now, with the potential for students to explore a full range of authoring of complex, multimedia texts, and with the tendency for much electronic text to break the boundaries of formal written conventions, all four language modes are coming closer together; the seamless robe of English teaching which practitioners have always envisaged has become a present reality.

These possibilities are likely to be seen by many English teachers as enhancing and extending what they have always been concerned to do. So too will the potential to connect with readers and writers across the world, to work with them and to take and use their texts. It is also certain that the audiences for which learners can write will be more varied, and that, as a consequence, teachers and their pupils will find it easier to identify authentic purposes for writing than they have to date.

At the time of writing it seems that the advent of the World Wide Web may mean that for the first time learners can publish on the same terms as everyone else, though it is important to recognize that there is a set of skills and disciplines which may be as difficult for some as handwriting is for others. Indeed, it is possible that the current generation of young people, who have grown up in the increasingly visual and animate age of television and computers, may themselves be teaching others about publishing in this medium. This development has come about for two reasons. First, students in schools can now have access to exactly the same compositional tools as everyone else, through the Internet. Second, there are differences in the gatekeeping which is associated with WWW publication. To date, unless the material is pornographic or seditious, the institutions or individuals operating to prevent anyone from publishing their own WWW pages are few, though China's policy of developing its own national 'intranet' has demonstrated what can be done. The increasing growth in intranets – or closed groups – may represent a move from the anarchic openness of the Internet towards the relative security of closure. For the moment, however, it is an opportunity that teachers and students are striving to exploit.

Perhaps the most problematic change that teachers will have to face is again to do with gatekeeping. The capacity for technology both to bring the adult world into the classroom and to take the classroom out into the adult world is likely to bring about changes in what can be taught and by whom.

Among the adults that this evolving information network will link up outside schools are, of course, many parents. They are going to use the information they gain through the network to assist their children in new ways, and may well develop increasing expectations of schools as a result of their own experiences. This development will in turn be fuelled by the recognition among publishing and media companies that there is a viable market emerging for home-based distance learning for children and adults. From a commercial point of view, the problem with open-ended packages, like word processors, is that by and large you can only sell someone one of these at a time. Packages that contain structured content, however, offer (like the TV documentary and the home video market) far more potential products to make up and sell into the home. But there will also be a demand from parents for instructional elements in this material to make up for their own perceived inability to provide such tutorial support themselves. It is therefore likely that either the information highway or, perhaps, CD-ROMs will bring into the home all kinds of learning materials.

Increasingly, the children themselves will become steadily more likely to have direct access to such a network at home, if not through computers, through cable networks. There have always been differences in the number of books and kinds of reading at home, and the evidence is that this has affected pupils' overall academic achievement as well as their reading ability. Yet it has always been society's expectation that it will be up to schools to take 'remedial' action. The situation changes dramatically, however, once homes are linked to the Internet, for it is then the school that risks becoming the text-starved location, not the home.

If the English curriculum is to deal with the kinds of texts that some children routinely encounter at home, the question about how to build upon pupils' reading and writing experiences outside school will be unavoidable. As the Internet enters the homes of those who own computers or of city dwellers who have cable, the diversity in the quantity and quality of the reading and writing experiences of individual children will grow. The principle of an *entitlement curriculum* will therefore become increasingly necessary and teachers will need to find out about their pupils' home experiences in order for reading and writing repertoires to be appropriately constructed to ensure a balanced experience for each individual.

A further consideration for the future will be a growing recognition that collective experience – in both writing and reading – should be seen as an entitlement, given the collaborative practices engendered by the new technologies. In principle this would be possible with a curriculum that requires range in the reading and writing experience rather than coverage of specific externally identified texts. There would be time for learners to develop the different skills and understandings that are demanded by working as individuals and as collaborators. In practice, understanding about how collaborative and individual reading and writing differ is in its infancy, and more needs to be known about these modes of working before they can be incorporated into a revised curriculum.

Perhaps the most far-reaching of all the implications raised by our reconsideration of the English curriculum is that of assessment. Some pupils routinely write using word processors. Evidence shows (Eklundh, 1994) that some people tackle writing entirely differently when they use a computer, but still children who have learned to write with computers are currently tested with paper and pencil. The same pupils may be writing and reading electronic texts outside school, yet there is currently little scope for assessing those achievements. As computer ownership grows, and with it disparities between individuals, it could well be that it becomes necessary for learners to have different starting points and to take different paths through the curriculum, but the current context in England, where course work and continuous assessment have been minimized, militates strongly against such possibilities. Further, while computers make possible the kinds of collaboration that are increasingly valued in the world at large and which therefore need to be recognized, the majority of assessment systems and mechanisms are designed to assess individual work. It seems important that educators should be able to recognize and validate those kinds of collaboration. However, there are already models in place which enable teachers to assess the individual's achievement within collaborative situations. For instance, the Primary Language Record has provided a workable model for recognizing and validating children's literacy experiences outside school. The National Oracy Project (Norman, 1992) demonstrated how valuable talk is as an assessment mechanism, and provides ways of approaching the problem of validating collaborative achievement. The work of the ACOT (Apple Classroom of Tomorrow) schools in the USA has been under way for ten years and is beginning to demonstrate that teachers who are familiar with the technology know how to plan for and assess the work of individuals within groups.

## Preparation for teaching the wider curriculum

One of the lessons of the Apple research is the importance for changing practice of the reflective teacher. In Chapter 4 we will be looking at the ways in which today's teachers have accommodated new ways of working in order to respond to the imperatives of an increasingly technological society. Before we do that, we conclude this section by considering the teachers whose work will be entirely conducted in an age of technology: how ready are they to take on the challenges that technology poses for the English curriculum?

Let us start with a description of how undergraduates in one Oxford college are studying for their English degree, the course that will qualify them to pursue a one-year Post Graduate Certificate of Education (PGCE) course that will prepare them for the classroom.

At university level, students of English literature are accustomed to considering questions about the provenance, destination and reception of texts, about single and multiple authorship, and about intertextuality and reader response. They do this both at a theoretical level and in their close reading of individual writers. On a typical day, for instance, in one Oxford college, the following classes are going on simultaneously, with three different sets of undergraduates.

A first-year group, studying modernism, are considering the question, 'who wrote *The Wasteland*?' with the facsimile manuscript in front of them. Analysing the text before and after Ezra Pound's intervention, they are asked to debate whether or not Eliot can be said to be the 'author' of *The Wasteland*, given the nature and extent of Pound's contribution. This question feeds appropriately into the thematic and formal concerns of a poem whose disconcerting medley of earlier and contemporary voices defeats the reader's metaphysical craving for 'origins' and 'unity'.

A second-year group, meanwhile, have met for a class in medieval literature, centring on the translation of part of the *Ancrene Wisse*, an early Middle English devotional manual in prose (author unknown), written for the guidance of English recluses. The class had been asked during the previous week to collaborate in producing a translation, each member of the group working on one paragraph before passing it on to the next person. The exercise has not only helped them to cover the ground quickly and enjoyably, it has also taught them about the responsibilities of joint authorship. This has historical relevance to the scribal culture which fostered the text under question, reminding them that there was a time when individual endeavours were subservient to communal ends, and when 'originality' did not enter the picture.

On the other side of the quad a group of third years are considering the quite different issues that are raised by texts written in the Romantic period, when authority was under question but originality at a premium. Their task is to analyse Wordsworth's *Prelude* in its three separate versions: the early one, only two books long, which has been recently discovered; the 13-book version which circulated among the poet's family and friends, but was never published in his lifetime; and the 14-book version, containing Wordsworth's lifelong revisions, which was published posthumously. The students are asked to consider what hidden agendas are disclosed in editorial or readerly preferences for one text over another: why should an earlier version be considered closer to 'creative origins', for instance, or why should a later version have more 'authority'? And are there really only three versions of the poem, if Wordsworth was revising it all his life? Doesn't each revision to the text constitute a new 'version'? Students are also encouraged to make cross-reference between versions, with their own evaluative preferences in mind, and to consider how their knowledge of the intended reader of each text affects its interpretation. (The unpublished 1805 text, for instance, was known throughout its life as the *Poem to Coleridge*: does the intimacy of its original audience affect critical judgements in any way?)

In all three classes, simple pedagogical tools are being used to stimulate critical or scholarly activity. What difference would it make if, instead of looking at xeroxes from the facsimile *Wasteland*, the first-year students were keyed into the Internet, studying the now available hypertext version? Or if the scribal community of second years in one college were able to consider and perhaps incorporate elements from the translations of their friends at other colleges? Or if the multiple variants of *The Prelude* were available on a single disk and it were possible to print out any part or combination of versions, at the flick of a switch? The potential for such teaching methods is there to be exploited, and it seems probable that their use would enable more sophisticated questions – or perhaps *different* questions, not as yet conceivable – to be asked.

(LN)

It has to be said, however, that not all undergraduate courses in English are like the one described above in providing experiences of reading which will develop the kinds of understandings about texts that are so necessary for teachers of English. Indeed, it is a major problem for those involved in initial teacher education that there is no very clear definition of what constitutes university English. With the increasing development of modular courses, the only thing that a group of trainees drawn from different universities and now embarking on a PGCE is likely to have in common is the possession of a degree in English. The range of their experience in reading for this degree will vary widely, as will their experience and expertise in information technology. In some ways this variety of experience may be seen as a strength, each member of a typical PGCE group making a specific individual contribution to the work of the group as a whole. But since those students starting on their courses at around the time this book is published will have teaching lives that will extend well into the twenty-first century, we need to ask questions about what they will require in their initial teacher education to prepare them for this.

At the very least, even to enable them to meet the demands of the existing National Curriculum, they will need to have more experience of language and media education than most university courses presently provide. They will also need to extend their experience of the reading of texts and their understanding of intertextuality at undergraduate level so as to lead to a further understanding about the creation of texts and about how to adapt their academic understanding to enable them to mediate this to the pupils they will be teaching. They will need to have developed skills in information technology so that they can use it confidently as a tool in their own work, both for the preparation of materials for the classroom and as a means of enabling learning by their pupils along the lines we explore in this book.

The actual picture of what we find when we look at the present population of initial teacher education students is a very mixed one indeed. In the academic year 1994–5, a small-scale investigation was conducted into the experience of, and attitudes towards, what we were still calling 'the new technologies' in three different university departments of education, and the results proved illuminating in their indication of the diversity that existed. It is of some significance that in all three institutions the lecturers teaching the courses were experienced and committed users of information technology in English teaching.

A questionnaire was devised to elicit the experience the students had had of information technology before beginning their courses. This showed that their school experience had given many of them no access to information technology, or if it had, they ignored it. Nearly 60 per cent claimed 'no use' at school and only 5 per cent reported 'considerable use'. Among the population of English graduates surveyed there was clearly some significant acquaintance with word processing, but with little else. However, their feelings were by no means negative; they were clearly interested in general in the implications of information technology for English teaching, but had little understanding of what these might entail. This was borne out by the administration of a further questionnaire at the end of the course. What seemed to have happened over the period was that the student teachers' awareness of possibilities had been increased. At the end of the course there was, for example, much more value placed upon screen-based texts than at the start. The same was true of their evaluation of pictures, though their perception of the value of printed books was in no way diminished as a consequence.

In terms, therefore, of their receptiveness to information technology in the curriculum and their capacity to develop new understandings and values in relation to text, this study of one cohort of students may be seen as encouraging. The extent to which this is achieved will, however, vary enormously given the increasingly school-based nature of initial teacher education. Colleges and universities are usually better equipped with information technology resources than schools, and it is important to do sufficient work to enthuse the prospective classroom teachers of English, while, at the same time, preventing unrealistic expectations of what they will currently find in practice in schools. Following the general argument that we have been advancing in this book, it seems likely that future generations of intending teachers will have had a much wider experience of the use of information technology than those currently starting their courses, but this is as much likely to have taken place in the home as in the school. The important task for teacher educators, in both colleges and schools, will be to explore how the information technology skills the students possess can be applied to the classroom in curriculum terms. This is why such approaches to texts as those employed in the Oxford undergraduate course are so significant; they provide a fertile ground in which the potential of information technology in the curriculum can be seeded and grow.

In considering the study just described, one experienced mentor commented:

> I was talking recently to an HMI who is responsible for drama and media studies across the country, and he said about 50 per cent of the schools he'd been in had no drama whatsoever. I think the case for media studies is even bleaker. The optimistic view would be that we could find some way of mirroring [how] the subject is currently dispersed in higher education and find a version of English studies which can encompass media studies, visual literacy [and] other kinds of literacies [together with] the technologies of representation that go with these kind of literacies . . . A large proportion of English work is about making available to children the resources for representation that they need to make the meanings that are important to them.

In the study, one of the PGCE students who had had least pre-course experience of the use of information technology was fortunate enough to be working with this particular mentor, but the school in which she was based was not especially rich in terms of information technology resources. Her attitude, at the end of her course, elicited through a personal interview, showed no lack of goodwill, though, understandably, it was still filled with logistical concerns about accessibility. Asked about her vision of the classroom of the future (2015 in fact), she replied:

> I don't know [about] thinking that far ahead. I think lots of things will still be the same. We will still have the role play and the group work, and their talking and

writing but I think information technology will contemplate [*sic*] more of a part and hopefully there will be more computers available to them so there's not the hassle of trying to book the computer room, they will be available in the class-rooms and every child will have access to one, so they can be used as and when the teacher wants to without having to have to try to book a computer room and it being full.

The need to bring together curriculum change and ease of access to the new technologies seems clear. What is also clear is the extent to which the good or ill experiences of school practice will inform the willingness of the new entrants to teaching to engage with the new technologies in their classrooms.

# 4 English in practice

The pressures on teachers are such that they might seem almost pathologically optimistic in attempting to take on new technologies in the face of class sizes of 35 plus, reduced budgets and increased societal expectations. Yet English teachers persist, knowing both intuitively and intellectually that the English curriculum is both changed and enhanced by the kind of understandings about information technology that children of the almost twenty-first century will so readily develop.

Disparities in information technology provision exist within counties, towns, areas. This is a problem now and will continue to be one for the future; indeed, it is likely to increase in its significance as societal expectations about young people's confidence and competence with new technologies grow. Nevertheless, while this should be no argument for ignoring the entitlement of all children to an education with information technology, it is the case that children in schools which are minimally equipped do not have to be excluded from a curriculum which prepares them for the twenty-first century. Indeed, teachers are already demonstrating what can be done at both ends of the resourcing continuum.

While teachers must continue to advance the arguments for appropriate resourcing of the English curriculum, they can feel confident that they are already cultivating the seeds for future ways of working. The flexibility of the primary classroom and the possibility of integrating language, information technology and other work makes good quality English and information technology easier to find there than in the secondary sector. The constraints of the current secondary National Curriculum in English, the weight of content and the unfamiliarity of teachers with ways of integrating information technology into examination courses have caused a reduction in the amount and range of work going on in English lessons between the early and mid-1990s: information technology has suffered along with media and drama. But the small steps which teachers have been taking have been made by those who are not being daunted by the scale of what might be done, who have been able to make connections between what they were previously doing and what the demands of information technology might suggest.

The purpose of this chapter is to demonstrate how we believe our framework for thinking about English connects with what teachers are already doing. We have adopted the device of presenting classroom examples as snapshots, as if through the eyes of a local education authority school inspector. Some are drawn from real life, others are 'faction' but based on genuine and possible classrooms. They are represented as a set of visit notes – one for each classroom. Our imaginary inspector's observation notes are followed in each case by her analysis of what she saw, focusing on issues we see as central to a reconsideration of English. The section concludes with an example contributed by one of our contributor writers in Australia, as a reminder that the issues explored in this book and the practices that are implicated are international.

## Visit 1: Infants making texts

The scene is a bustling infant classroom. All round the room children's work is displayed: some hand-written, some word-processed along with some commercially produced material. There are lots of story books around which children are handling, inspecting and reading. The children are involved in making their own books using the commercial versions as models. They have become familiar with many of the books through their classroom activities and have shared them with the teacher and other adults.

There are three old, but functional, BBC/Acorn computers in the classroom, which are not used for other information technology work in the school, but which are fine for producing words to be printed. Different groups and individuals are working in different ways. Some are pretty handy at generating their own text at the screen, individually or in pairs; others are supported by the teacher or a helper acting as scribe writing on to paper. Others are putting their stories on to tape. There aren't enough BBCs for everyone to have enough time to write at the keyboard, but they do take turns to edit the text already input from the scribed or taped versions by some older 'assistant'. They can choose to do this individually or with a friend or helper, depending on their skills. The printer is in another classroom, so children receive their print-outs in subsequent lessons. Occasionally, the printer (black and white) is available in the classroom, so that they can witness the process of transforming screen text into hard copy.

When they have their own words in glorious dot matrix, they cut and paste the bits of text on to card and hand-draw the pictures and covers, which are then spiral-bound for inclusion in the class library – after mum or dad has seen this first edition publication of course! One child who has a computer at home has produced the illustrations on her computer, printed them on a colour printer and brought them in to be stuck alongside the black and white words. She explains to the others what she did, and they compare their own products with the commercial books which were their original stimulus.

*Learning to make texts*

The use of tape recorders from which to transcribe the stories is labour-intensive, but allows unconfident writers to see how ideas can be transformed into print, as they receive, respond to, modify and enhance their own texts. Their readings of the books provided in this lesson will inform their making of more complex texts when these children have access to scanners, multimedia systems, video cameras and colour printers: they will be able to scan print texts and modify them, pastiche television texts and create picture books which compare well with commercial products. These advanced activities all build on the early foundations about making texts and authorial choice.

*Learning about authorship*

These pupils have fulfilled the teacher's initial expectations of working collaboratively to generate texts from their individual narratives and the finished books are thus jointly authored texts. The teacher talked with the children about how their books differed from many of those they had been reading, since the books they used as their models are mostly single authored. Particular books generated new understandings about the publishing process, and about the decisions available to writers, editors and illustrators, and the constraints on them. Although the teacher did not deal explicitly with the concept of gatekeeping, it is embodied in the teacher as editor and facilitator and is thus highly visible to the young writers.

*Learning about texts*

In their comparison of their own books with those by writers like Hutchins, Sendak, Hughes and McKee, there was discussion about the relationship between print and image, and about the grammar of pictures. Their interpretations moved into the realms of language study, media studies and design study. The children were well able to see how illustrators signal, for example, parental irritation (Bernard's parent's closed eyes when they speak to him in *Not Now, Bernard* by David McKee) or the contrast between dream and reality (the sepia and colour pages in *Come Away from the Water Shirley* by John Burningham). They were able to detect the subplots in *You'll Soon Grow into Them, Titch* by Pat Hutchins, and enthusiastically point out the signs. These understandings, often surprising to adults, are signs of children's ability to read texts at various levels. The structure of these texts challenges the linear construction of many pre-twentieth-century texts and reflects the age of televisual literacy and the experimental novel.

*Assessing the learning*

During the making process and in the light of the final product, it was significant that the teacher was unable to assess the achievement in writing of any of the pupils, because she found it difficult to identify and describe who had contributed what. However, during the class discussions, she was able to note down some important understandings demonstrated by the individuals who spoke. She found this discussion a useful basis for identifying what she would be looking for when the children next worked in a similar way.

## Visit 2: Using today's texts in the community

Visit to a nursery school in an economically depressed area of a small town. The headteacher has been very active in generating and promoting a parent and child reading project with a difference. She showed me this copy of an article from the local paper.

### Blooming good results in nursery

*When Sandy Phillips set up the CHIPS scheme in September 1994 she was determined to succeed. The Cherry Hill Parents Scheme, based at Sandy's nursery school, was designed to give the mums of her toddler charges easy access to word processors, the Internet and the world of work. Lots of women wanted to get back to work to improve their qualifications, but found it difficult to fit a college course into their other commitments. So in conjunction with the local College of Technology and Art, and several departments in the county council, the CHIPS became a reality.*

*Paul Timpson of the college said, 'We knew there were lots of potential students in Cherry Hill who simply couldn't fit a conventional "Return to Learn" course into their lives. CHIPS is accessible and user friendly, and we now have about twenty students on travel and tourism, word-processing and care courses who first tried their hand at CHIPS.'*

*So, Sandy has no need to fish for compliments, CHIPS is a roaring success. If you've ever wanted to know how it feels to surf the Internet, or just want to call up on screen a copy of the newspaper for your date of birth, pop along to Cherry Hill, where it's CHIPS with everything!*

In addition to giving adults access to skills, the computers are linked into local information services and to the Internet. For six hours a day, local people can use the CHIPS room to write job applications, create party invitations or keep track of their bills. They can look up details of local councillors and send them e-mail messages, and they can do research using the most up-to-date encyclopaedias and databanks. They can log into a wide range of medical and childcare programmes too. The head told me that one user had found the CancerHelp facility at just the right time. She had told her how after her father was told he had cancer, she was too worried to talk to the doctor, but that she had found CancerHelp easy to use, and learned much more than she felt she would take in during a consultation at a busy hospital.

Elsewhere in the nursery, parents and toddlers are enjoying books and songs together in a preschool reading group, and some mums and dads stay on when their children move into the nursery class for an hour's lesson to improve their own maths and English skills.

*Establishing a context for learning*

Although this initiative is the only one of its kind being explored by this local authority, it is a living example of how multi-agency developments can be effective. The head of the school is a key motivator, being the familiar interface between the local authority and the parents in the area. Without her and the accessible location, the project would be less successful and the practical problems about access and staffing the base would be insurmountable. It is a small base: only one room, a smattering of hardware and a part-time technician adviser, but it exists and is being used. Funding is jointly provided by social services, education and a community development fund. Local politicians are very keen to support and to be seen to be involved. Spending by the community development fund is closely watched by elected members and is targeted at those wards where there is the greatest social need.

The social implications of this use of information technology and language are powerful: it impacts on early literacy in that parents are more confident users and modellers of language, and the scheme interfaces with reading clubs. Adult literacy and learning are enhanced by ease of access and ready progression to further education. The unthreatening venue of the nursery school provides a base which is also a transition between a domestic context and an educational one.

*Learning to use texts*

The adult learners in this context have access, as individuals or pairs, to written language, graphics and computer generated sound via the Internet and disk-based information sources. The gatekeeper for this information is the county council, which provides the reference sources and a filtered Internet access. The forms of text available to users are predominantly multiply authored, such as commercially produced CD-ROMs, Internet pages and the databases provided by the local council; in contrast, the texts generated by the users themselves are usually singly authored. Users treated the information they found at the base as they would treat information from a library or Citizen's Advice Bureau.

The range of purposes was varied: for information, for communication and exploration. The potential audiences are equally varied, though initially they are likely to be relatively close at hand, for example enabling interaction with local politicians.

## Visit 3: Authentic activity with technology and texts

The first time you visit a primary school on an army camp site it is a strange experience: you have to phone in advance, sign in at the gatehouse, flanked by heavily armed and booted young men and women, drive between the tanks and boilerhouses with an immense pass card stuck to the windscreen, only to happen across a completely normal, cheerful, busy primary school behind the barbed wire fences. Here, Year 7 pupils from two schools are working on a five-day simulation called 'Police: language in evidence'. The visiting pupils are from a small village primary four miles away.

In teams of six, mixed by ability, gender and school, pupils investigate a range of incidents generated in real time by a computer. They confidently use, through-out the week, cameras, tape recorders, video cameras, intercoms, word proces-sors and databases. They interview, among others, the commanding officer, the bonded warehouse manager, a train driver, the crossing warden and the guard-house officers. They work comfortably alongside the camp photographer, a ser-geant in the military police, new teachers and pupils. As Lady Blyston, I am interviewed by two 'officers' in uniforms they had made the previous week. They each make notes of my answers to prepared questions, and write them up collaboratively into a report, which they compare with the report written by others who have interviewed Lord Blyston, played by a visiting teacher.

By the end of the week, they have engaged purposefully in hundreds of inter-actions with dozens of individuals on a wide range of real and realistic problems and tasks. The teacher, having been set up each day as the station commander, is able to intervene to prompt individuals' progress and to make assessments of pupils' speaking and listening in a range of contexts.

The military police sergeant is so pleased with the work and with the re-sponses of the children that he offers to come to any school in the county to help set up and run a similar project. I think I'll take him up on that.

(Work seen in Warwickshire LEA)

*Developing critical literacy*

This simulation is tricky to set up, but well worth the investment. Hardware was borrowed from around the school and some equipment was loaned by the visiting school. Children used the school cameras, but they were also able to handle the professional versions and to use the photographs from both and to compare results. The intercoms were baby listeners, toy walkie-talkies and professional equipment demonstrated by the military police. Pupils were quick to discern qualitative differences between the various bits of equipment, and between the products created by themselves and those by the professionals, but all were willing and able to suspend disbelief for the purposes of the simulation. They had first-hand experience of a range of technologies which simulate the work of investigative officers. Cameras recorded the scenes of crimes and yielded opportunities for close observation, analysis, descriptive writing and discussion. They saw vividly the differences between images of the same scene taken by a point-and-press camera, a Hasselblad and the school video, and could analyse the choices made by different users about framing, angle and position. They discussed the differences between interviewing a suspect face-to-face and on the intercom, commenting on body language and eye contact. This debate was developed by recording some interviews on video and analysing the relationships between facial and vocal expression. In these contexts, they were developing their visual critical faculties and their media awareness.

The databases were authored by the simulation's designer but purported to be the records created by fictional police officers. The data were loaded by pupils as they interviewed witnesses and suspects. As they wanted to confirm times, places, responses and details of observations, they searched the database using key words so as to compare reports and to confirm or reject their hypotheses. This interaction with a database within a realistic context allowed them to explore the functions of such a program and to realize its potential and limitations.

*Authentic purposes*

Social development and oracy were also part of the planned learning: pupils had to interact with a range of unfamiliar adults, usually seen in positions of authority. The school serves a shifting community, with children who often find it difficult to concentrate for long periods, and who find it hard to set up relationships quickly. This activity kept every one of them riveted for a full week: they talked about it at home, parents came in to see what was happening and the imaginative frame created and developed over time provided a secure context in which dramas, role plays, speculations, hypotheses and presentations were the norm for pupils who find these language uses difficult to grasp without solid preparation. The fact that they worked with pupils from another local authority school in their final year before moving to secondary school was deliberately set up to give them contact with children from another type of community with whom they would be mixing after transfer.

The program central to the experience generates instructions to the pupils who form the day's duty team at preset moments. At the start of the day, pupils have to log on to see what the fictional night duty team has left on file in the way of unfinished investigations, new information and incidents which they have to decide to follow up or ignore. In the middle of their discussion, new information starts to arrive, since the program is designed to generate particular information, some significant, some red herrings, at set points in time after it is set running for the school day. Pupils are motivated, have real discussions about real decisions for action and write a wide range of 'real' texts for realistic audiences. The forms with which the pupils work are clearly related to forms from the real context emulated in the simulation; the purposes are more varied, being related to the pupils' own needs to persuade, explore, inform, entertain and express.

*Language learning*

In terms of language development, during the week the pupils wrote notes, logs, reports, interview transcripts, accounts of incidents, speculative summaries of alternative possibilities and flow charts of events and motivations, and took themselves very seriously. They were learning how language can be slippery, how words can mean various things, how precise language is necessary for particular circumstances and how to construct it.

## Visit 4: Reading against CD-ROM texts

A Year 6 class in a multilingual primary school is organized into mixed ability groups. Within each group children are paired so that those who are not proficient in English are supported by another pupil who is able to speak the language. For this half-term period there are two CD-ROM players available in the classroom, with one colour printer. The machines are in the reading corner so that children may browse through both books and CD-ROMs in a similar way.

Before introducing the CD-ROMs into the classroom, the teacher spent time developing word-processing skills to make sure they could complete the task she was about to set. Initially, two children who were confident CD-ROM users acted as 'trouble-shooters', helping others in the class when the teacher wasn't available, but the children are by now reasonably proficient, so their help is not needed very often.

The initial task encouraged children to 'browse' through an encyclopaedia. Each pair was then asked to find some text and a picture that related to the class topic so that they could produce a 'Did you know?' book.

You can tell when a new picture has been discovered on the encyclopaedia the children are working with: there is great excitement and the news has to be shared (immediately!) with everyone else. The teacher comments that the children had high expectations of the CD-ROM, many of them believing that it would be an extension of the interactive computer games they had experienced at home and that there would be much action. In that respect their expectations have not been met but they appear undaunted.

It has been made clear to them that they are not simply to print out chunks of the encyclopaedia, but to read through the text and edit out the parts they do not understand or that they think are unnecessary. The teacher tells how this immediately gives the children power over the text. Most still find it easier to print out the text and to do their editing from the print-out (which also makes time management of the computer easier). But whereas, previously, they regarded the information in the program as 'gospel', the children are now taking greater control over the text on screen when they revisit the CD-ROM.

The teacher comments:

> I noticed an interesting gender difference: boys seem less preoccupied with the end product of their work than girls – they spend most of their time moving about the pages and at the last minute save whatever page they're at. Girls seem to be more discerning, spending time choosing the 'right' information and editing.
>
> At the end of the session I observed the children talking as a class about what they had been doing. Amongst other things they commented that the

pages of information on the CD-ROM program are not set out in an interesting way and should include a greater variety of diagrams, tables, charts – because that was what the children had chosen to put on their pages!

(Adapted from a case study by Bet Lowe, Redbridge LEA)

## Developing critical literacy

This unit of work had been set up to help pupils to develop their skills as critical readers of electronic text, with the teacher as the explicit gatekeeper who vetted the texts she made available. As a result of the work, pupils were more able to question the veracity of the information contained on the CD-ROM, once they found that they could manipulate it. This was not to encourage them to lose faith in all recorded information, which would be anarchic and retrograde, but to help them to be more critical readers of all kinds of text. Throughout, this needed careful handling by the teacher, and a clear idea of the learning she wanted to take place, asking questions like 'Who wrote this bit?', 'How do you know that's true?', 'How could you check it out?', 'How could you present that in a more simple way for our book without distorting it?'

Both boys and girls had initially unrealistic expectations of the technology, believing from the hype of advertising that they would contain all the information that they wanted on everything, that they would be 'all singing, all dancing' and that their half-formed vision of what they wanted to produce would be magically created at the touch of a key. One of the purposes of the exercise was to show what a CD-ROM can and cannot do, and how the technology can be used for one's own purposes, rather than uncritically accepting the 'givens' of the gatekeeper, but the teacher was careful not to put a ceiling on the pupils' speculations about what future technological devices might be able to do.

## Learning about texts and authorship

The process of adapting the print-outs for their own 'Did you know?' books gave pupils insights into how texts are created: they were able to see that choices had been made by the originators of the texts about images, charts, words and diagrams, and that these did not necessarily correspond with their own preferred choices. They could see how the encyclopaedia had been written for a relatively wide audience, but that their editing of the information allowed them to target what they included more precisely for their own school and peer group, taking into account the need for more visual representation for those class members whose English was less confident than that of others.

The shared purpose of the class book was a familiar enterprise, and they already understood the notion of shared authorship in this context, but they came to a clearer understanding of multiple authorship of commercial texts by comparing perceptions about style and presentation, and by observing the sheer bulk of information in the encyclopaedia, which could only reasonably have been created collaboratively by several contributors. They could also see that their own book was relatively uniform – it was a coherent single text, as they had structured it, whereas the CD-ROM was interactive and provided multiple texts for readers to create, including sounds, music and moving models as well as static diagrams and print.

There is unlikely to be time for this kind of work to take place again during the pupils' primary school life, but as access to CD-ROMs becomes more commonplace, and as the range and complexity of texts they encounter increases, this early awareness of texts and authorship will be developed.

*Developing and assessing reading and information skills*

To achieve any success, pupils had to use and to develop appropriate information handling skills and quite high order reading skills. Since pupils were working in pairs, the teacher could make assessments of their contributions and developing understandings, particularly useful in the mixed language ability pairings. The difference between the boys' and the girls' approach to the task was interesting and raised many questions: the girls seemed more willing to take cognizance of the potential readership and to select and change information and presentation to suit. This gave the teacher evidence of the learning processes she wanted to assess, whereas the boys' consuming interest in the workings of the program afforded her fewer insights into their understandings about audience, authorship and editorial choices.

## Visit 5: Out of school learning and literary studies

A visit was made to a secondary school, to see a Year 10 class preparing presentations for each other about significant aspects of information technology texts. They have been working on *Pride and Prejudice*, and have used a range of print, media and electronic resources over the four weeks since they started reading it.

This part of their work on *Pride and Prejudice* will generate material for their examination language coursework and will be used for an assessment of speaking and listening. Other elements of the module will provide assignments for their literature folders.

The work begins with a class discussion of the various texts they use at home and school: teletext, computer games, CD-ROM, television, interactive video, radio news, electronic communication and the World Wide Web. In groups they identify which forms have provided them with, or could have provided them with, information to support their study of *Pride and Prejudice*. A recent TV film adaptation has generated a lot of interest nationally, which helps them to see how a print text can be adapted and can spawn a range of new media texts. There is a lively discussion about the cult surrounding the actor playing Darcy which is evident in the popular press, and about the way that the making of the film has become a source of interest in itself. An aunt has been on a coach tour to the various great houses used in the film, a family watched a programme which recorded the making of the film and another had visited Jane Austen's house in Winchester. One pupil brought in her dad's book, written by the producer, which chronicled the decisions taken from having the original idea and trying to get finance, to final screening, including interviews and logs by costume designers, dance historians, actors, facsimile documents written by the musical director and continuity staff, extracts from the screen play showing various editorial changes and conversations with ordinary people whose lives and villages had been turned upside down by the arrival of a film crew. One had printed out the latest contributions to a discussion group that she had found on the World Wide Web.

Pupils are asked to make a presentation comparing the benefits of the different forms for supporting their work on *Pride and Prejudice*. One of the options is to suggest how a form like the World Wide Web site could be developed to support work on *Pride and Prejudice*, including contributors from various parts of the world giving cultural and historical perspectives on the novel. Another is to consider the content and structure of a CD-ROM for researching the novel. Pupils less familiar with a range of electronic texts are able to work with those who are, or may consider work in media with which they are comfortable, such as TV and radio. They have access to a small number of networked computers in the English area, and each group creates a shared file, accessible through the network to the rest of the class, to log its planning and thinking.

When they make their presentations they will be asked to address in particular three questions:

- Who wrote the text?
- How was the text written?
- Why was the text written?

They will also be asked to address the environmental, ethical, moral, cultural and social issues raised by such information technology applications.

After the presentation pupils will write evaluations of the texts they encountered when studying *Pride and Prejudice*.

## Building on out-of-school learning

This is a unit of work which is familiar in kind, but is designed to draw on experiences which pupils are bringing from home and elsewhere rather than necessarily being offered solely by the school. The media to which the school has been able to give access are CD-ROMs (encyclopaedias for general research as well as one specific to the novel), World Wide Web pages, video copies of television programmes, an audio tape of a radio adaptation, newspaper articles and features, commercially produced educational publications and various print editions of the novel.

The representational systems and modes of transmission are various: speech and music on the audio tapes, writing and images in the print media, performance drama and dance in the video versions, computer generated graphics and interactive text on the CD-ROMs, but students have few problems accessing information from any of these. Neither do they have problems with the wide range of forms represented: the linear novel and the non-linear arrangement of data in the CD-ROM encyclopaedia; the stable verbal form of the scripted audio play and the wide ranging and ephemeral class discussions; or the commercial notes provided by the teacher and the shared, interactive word-processed files each group creates to log its thinking.

## *Learning about authorship*

The pupils' analyses of how various text forms could help them to understand Jane Austen's novel show that they see how texts might be multiply authored: Jane Austen's original bears an individual stamp on which later editors make little impression, but the book about the making of the film is an overtly multi-voiced, multi-form text edited by Sue Birtwhistle, the producer, who acts as a kind of compere providing commentary and linkages. The electronic texts range from the multi-authored e-mail conversations to the monographs on Empire line corsetry included in the encyclopaedias. The pupils were also able to demonstrate an enhanced understanding of how a classic work of literature is not an artefact in isolation, but is part of a web of texts and meanings created over time and across the globe. Interestingly, the purposes of the texts encountered in this unit are similarly varied: the novel is designed to entertain; the encyclopaedias are designed to inform; the newspaper articles and the producer's book are a form of infotainment; and their own presentations are essentially explorations in which pupils can express opinions.

## *Assessing the individual*

These pupils understand clearly the imperative to produce single authored single texts for their coursework folders, and are sympathetic to the teacher's need to be able to identify individual achievement in written work. They also understand that oral assessments can be made in more flexible contexts, and make sure that group members have an opportunity to demonstrate their skills during the presentation. In their presentations and written evaluations, all pupils demonstrate, to varying degrees, an understanding of the combinations and continua which are available to writers, editors and readers.

## Conclusion

These five snapshots of classrooms are not offered as a panacea, or as a model of an ideal curriculum, but as examples of what can be done by teachers who have a clear idea about how information technology enhances language learning and critical literacy. The broader curriculum for English contains, of course, much that is not here and much that can be taught well in a classroom without any electronic equipment. But pupils in schools today will be adults in the next millennium, and a vast amount of the information with which they will have to deal will be multi-authored and multimedia. Truly to comprehend a text, a reader has to understand something of how it came into being and the ways in which it might be read. That is why the Year 2 teacher is helping her young authors to deconstruct the picture books, in the same way that the Year 10 teacher encourages older students to analyse the production and authorship of texts in a range of media. The interrelationship of composing and analysing is recognized in the structure of the art and music curriculum and in the reading/writing duality of the English curriculum. The problem with early media studies was the cerebral nature of the critique – students were not enabled to learn by making, or to grasp the subtleties of tone or juxtaposition by having a go at a pastiche. The new technologies make the deconstruction of texts in classrooms a real possibility, and give students a critical and creative vocabulary which acknowledges the technologies with which they are familiar in their lives out of school.

Some of the teachers in the snapshots had difficulty with assessment of individual achievement when the product was a collaborative enterprise. In fact, those initial anxieties soon evaporate when the quality of talk and the assessments possible through talk are the focus. Talk is the observable evidence of the processes of learning which are manifest as a result of collaborative work, in ways which individual work cannot reveal. Talk is evanescent and difficult to catch, but it is also where learners can take risks and experiment, whereas in their writing they may be cautious and safe. In the Year 6 situation, the teacher fully exploited the need to talk, forcing new learning by structuring the pairings, and planning the assessments she wanted to make.

All the snapshots show children and young people struggling to make meaning, both of others' texts and in creating their own. In the CHIPS scheme, it is adults who are catching up with the learning their children will take for granted. Only in the act of creating and manipulating text for authentic purposes of understanding or communication does one really learn how to use language and how it is being used. Every lesson described in this chapter is a language lesson, within which the learners are motivated to interact by the context in which they are placed. On their own neither the technology nor the activity is sufficient – the teacher must have a coherent view of how language learning takes place and know how to intervene to develop individual skills and capabilities.

Let us finish this chapter with a contribution from Australia. Just as the Year 6 pupils working with the CD-ROM were working in a context where the choices they made about tone and lay-out affected the meaning they wished to communicate, so these pupils are keen to explore the technology in their search for meaning. Here, too, as in the 'Police: language in evidence' simulation, the sense of audience and purpose, whether real or imagined, is a powerful frame and motivator.

---

Working in pairs, a class of older students produced a personalized interactive picture book for a much younger child. The older students first talked with the younger child, finding out his or her preferences in story lines, characters and settings. The Year 9 students then worked on a computer-based interactive picture book which had the following features: Hypercard was used to create animated illustrations; characters in the text introduced themselves verbally, spoke to one another and directly addressed the reader by name; a photograph of the reader was scanned and reproduced in the dedication at the start of the 'book'; and the responses of the reader were sought during the initial development of the story line. At the end of the project readers gave writers feedback on the aspects of the book they most enjoyed. Writers also studied the produced texts.

The project entailed various kinds of learning for all students. The issue of using appropriate language in the text generated much discussion within pairs and prompted worthwhile follow-up discussions with the intended reader. In producing their texts, students worked collaboratively, not only within pairs, but also with able students acting as mentors and instructors for others, especially in explaining how to create the animations, solve technical problems and tighten story lines. In each pair students had to reach a consensus on all decisions, with pairs working in quite contrasting ways. For example, some pairs used collaborative drawing, while in other pairs one student drew a character throughout the text. Many students felt the necessity for their own texts to differ from other emerging ones, and this prompted extended exploration of communicative options and technical innovation. This exploration of technical possibilities to enhance communicative effect, as many teachers have noted, is a major learning opportunity in this kind of project. The readers in this project, both young and old, were learning first-hand about the pleasures and opportunities of new technologies for texts and reading.

**(VP)**

---

# 5 Into the twenty-first century

In this chapter we take the bold step of future gazing, knowing that in ten years' time, if not earlier, we may regret having set these words in print. If any one part of this book is published on the World Wide Web, it should be this. Were it to be so we would be free to change and add to it as we re-cast our speculations to build upon the realities that emerge between now and the future they are intended to suggest.

Future gazing is a speculative and absorbing game for the writers but, for the readers, perhaps only convincing if a balance is achieved between the exhilaration of some possible improvements (imagine what radical transformations of everyday life a Victorian whisked into the late twentieth century would marvel at, and how similarly improbable future changes are likely to be) and the likelihood that many aspects of educational life will remain difficult, contentious and short of the ideal (imagine with what rapid ease that same Victorian could identify a school as a school for all its appearance of modernity). We need to acknowledge that many forces will change the nature of English, and that information technology is only one, but it is nevertheless likely to be an influence that becomes deep and pervasive because of its capacity to alter the nature of our understanding of text.

There is not room, in one chapter, to explore the full complexity of likely changes to all aspects of, and versions of, the subject 'English'. We shall, therefore, focus for the most part on literary studies, activities which have come to be the centrally defining ones for secondary school English in the United Kingdom at least. As Green (1990) argues, one of the results of an essentially literary curriculum is that writing is conceived of not as unimportant, but as nevertheless falling short of the supremacy of reading. In an age when digitized text becomes the norm, an assumed background, then that norm is very likely to influence the learnt responses which support literary kinds of reading and writing. 'Writing back' will become so habitual a response that school students will be inclined, by their culture, to see literary texts as interesting and worthy of study to the degree that they are changeable, that they can accept, incorporate or resist attempts on the reader/writer's part to modify their form or substance.

English will remain a contentious subject, but some lessons will be seen as exemplifying its best possibilities: they will both appeal to the learners and be seen to derive from concerns to fulfil the complex demands which learners will be under in coping with a shifting and puzzling world. Below is an example of one kind of lesson, simply imagined as part of an exercise in projecting how some present ways of working might be extended once the hardware is in place. It is given here as a fiction, a vignette in the form of a set of research notes from a visitor's collection of impressions. This device is used simply because it enables the writer's freedom to imagine a future without having to sound endlessly repetitive about the reader's having to imagine it.

---

As to its appearance, this English classroom was more like an art room or studio. The prototype for this classroom was developed in the late twentieth century in the seemingly unpromising territory of Bradford, but all the compelling images, visual and verbal, were put there by the teacher, clearly with the aid of some exhibition technologies, borrowed from that city's superb museum of film, photography and television. In this classroom, in a comprehensive school, the images were put in place by the students. The class was given a 'learning-environment enhancement project' halfway through the first term, and had to decide how to transform and then deploy poems and other forms of visual and verbal metaphors, mainly on paper and card perhaps, but also on screen displays. These 'environment enhancement projects' have enjoyed a brief vogue at a time when it has become apparent that school interiors are under-funded and, yet again, rhetoric substitutes for resources. A small increase in departmental funding has, by administrative intention, meant that students around the school have had their labour used as a substitute for that of professional decorators. This English teacher made the most of the opportunity anyway. We saw digitally painted scenes – images in colour and shape – based on phrases from Carol Rumens's poem 'Star Whisper', wherein breath turns to ice in the coldest place on earth. These appeared on screens mounted in the corridor walls.

**Star Whisper**

*for Eugene Dubnov*

> If you dare breathe out in Verkhoyansk
>> You get the sound of life turning to frost
>> As if it were an untuned radio,
>>> A storm of dust.
>
> It's what the stars confess when all is silence
> – Not to the telescopes, but to the snow.
> It hangs upon the trees like silver berries
>> – Iced human dew.

Imagine how the throat gets thick with it,
How many versts there are until the spring,
How close the blood is, just behind the lips
      And tongue, to freezing.

Here, you can breathe a hundred times a minute,
And from the temperate air still fail to draw
Conclusions about whether you're alive
      – If so, what for.

The central image, of breath becoming ice, was one which the students took to well because they wondered how it was that a twentieth-century poet could have foreseen the significance of the spoken word (on the breath, perhaps) transformed by the medium into a visible product. Several, incidentally, had tried to compress into a single screen image the idea of a radio-telescope deaf to the secrets it was designed to capture. When the computer suggested, as a caption, the words 'In them hath he set a tabernacle for the sun; there is neither speech nor language, but their voices are heard among them' this was rejected by the students as some kind of aberrant, ungrammatical nonsense, inexplicable, and the incident was over before the teacher had a chance to see what the computer had done.

In place of the image of the deaf telescope, found hard to portray, most concentrated instead on the breath turning to ice, an idea made possible by the use of a painting program, with dynamics, wherein the breath is made to freeze as it moves from left to right. Several students wanted to extend the idea of breath, and make words on the screen metamorphose into ice. ('Ah, but which words, kids, and do we hear them or just see them?' That took some deciding in the groups.)

The students have seen computers routinely turn their dictation into print, after a certain fine-tuning at the keyboard. Now the breathed word has been re-imaged as an element of nature. All this re-contexting has meant that writing and speaking have at times become rather bewilderingly (con)fused, but the teacher's demand to illustrate a collection of poems and prose passages which themselves dwelt on the word as image brought a certain clarification to the relationship of spoken word to written, and of written word to picture. One of the students, trawling for ideas, brought from her net an antique document called *English 5–16* ('They left education at 16?'), but her teacher was quick to show that earlier generations had wondered how the spoken word related to the written, a question by no means fully answered yet, but one which was going to be explored by the voice-to-print technology later in the year.

What this vignette points to is the capacity of computers to help translate one medium into another, and, in a way, to elide reading and response. It also points to the capacity of context to influence interpretation. In this episode the poem has come to be seen as a statement about the nature of language; this slant is given greater persuasiveness if other texts, to do with language, have been placed on the circuits in such a way as to be easily found alongside the Rumens poem.

When it comes to reading and intertextual relationships, future generations of English teachers are going to have to do much to construct frameworks for interpretation, to build contexts through comparisons and extended reading. They will have guides to action from our own times if they wish, such as Andrew Stibbs's (1991) *Reading Narrative as Literature*, but the difficulty will be to balance two rather different approaches. Teachers might on the one hand abandon individual students to the whole world – the global mass of internetted webs – or, on the other, create a local environment, a restricted territory, wider than most forms of current school library provision, but essentially controlled and listable. You could see this as a debate between open access and conscientiously arranged sets of selections. This debate could well be contentious territory at more than just pedagogical and psychological levels. It could well be that some countries will prefer the idea of free access as ultimately more informative and others will prefer the more limited focus (via such things as the CD-ROM), because it ties the technological arrangement to state-wide uniform curriculums.

A second vignette makes the point about the effects of these kinds of choices.

---

**Time: the future**

**Place: a classroom**

Clare handed over the slip of paper reluctantly. It consisted of one line only and read: 'http://high.csv.city.ac.uk/WWW/Eng/Hamlet/sjt.html'.

'It's not quite finished, Miss. Can't I give it in tomorrow?'

'No,' her English teacher replied, glancing at it as she added it to her pile. 'You know as well as I do that it'll never be finished. Today is the deadline and you'll have to be satisfied with it as it is.' She turned her attention to the rest of the class. 'Any more course work pieces?'

Some handed in paper – two to three thousand word essays by the look of them – others disks – multimedia presentations. They had been working on the *Hamlet* assignment for three weeks now. 'Is Shakespeare multicultural?' was the broad question they had started with. But each pupil refined it to generate his or her own particular focus.

The difference between Clare's piece and the disk- and paper-based presentations of her classmates was that she could not guarantee that the teacher would be reading the same text that she had been working on at home the previous night. Hers was presented on the World Wide Web and, within it, Clare had created links with other texts from across the world. She had incorporated images of costume designs, critiques of productions, brief clips from movies of *Hamlet* from Russia and Japan and an on-line discussion. And she knew that these were liable to be changed at any time by their originators. What difference, she wondered, might those changes make to her final grade?

---

In both vignettes it is clear that students have to act as readers, writers, searchers, editors, those who understand text forms and the characteristics of the media with which they choose to work. Clare's problem, and her teacher's, is in part connected with the instability of electronic text and in part to do with individuality and private ownership. In both the first vignette and the second, the teacher's critical questions for the class have to do with the reception of the texts into some kind of moral framework or interpretative community. Might both the shared nature of documents on the Web, and the focus on reception into larger frameworks than those contained in the immediate awareness of the class, put out of the teacher's mind questions about what particular parts of a play or poem mean to the alert, purely individual and sensitive reader?

We need a third vignette.

---

**Time: the future**

**Place: a study-bedroom in a student's house**

The student, August, works alone, at a desk which houses a computer. He registers, on a database page, that he is working at home today. Tuesdays are elective days for those in his sets for English and maths. This arrangement, in its infancy, did create the odd class-management problem; no one could be utterly certain that the students were working at home, but gradually the problems became as well solved as any other attendance problems, and such was the pressing need to save fuel and keep air clean that it was desirable to avoid even commuter journeys to school whenever possible.

August will work at home, and send in his results, by e-mail, by 15.30 at the latest. He selects this time in one of four preset boxes. All students are eventually awarded a time management grade dependent upon the gap between estimated time and the actual arrival of the work. This device is regarded by the students as an enormous joke, but most play the game, secretly believing that it will help them in the world of work.

After this he downloads, by prior arrangement, a folder of poems and selects one by Gerard Manley Hopkins, entitled 'Inversnaid'. This is the first verse:

The darksome burn, horseback brown,
His rollrock highroad roaring down,
In coop and in comb the fleece of his foam
Flutes and low to the lake falls home.

August finds this hard work to read, but after two attempts to make sense of it unaided he chooses to hear it read aloud by optional voice circuits held in the file. No one has any way of monitoring what our student is up to; this is a self-imposed discipline which he follows here, but the first frustrating (silent) readings were not entirely in vain, because he suddenly understands on the first voiced reading what had puzzled him initially, namely that the word 'falls' is what the darksome burn does. 'Falls' functions as a verb, but had offered itself on first view as a noun, the second half of the term 'lake falls'. The actor–reader employed on the file makes a clear break after the word 'Flutes' and another, but shorter, break after the word 'falls', and in these breaks helps to clarify the rather complex grammatical structure of the first verse. August's instructions are to annotate his response to any poem about the environmental theme which his class had been following in English lessons, devoted to understanding something of the significance of remote places as more than just body-testing arenas.

This is not the most successful theme which the teacher has embarked on with his class, but something he said about spirituality, isolation and their projections on to landscapes struck a chord with the 16-year-old August, who seems defeated in his attempts to find himself on the top of Whernside alone, ever. Even at seven on a May morning the athletes pound the ground. (He was an odd bod, this English teacher who dared to use words like 'spirituality', but he got away with it partly because he was a superbly adept rock-climber.) August finds himself pleasantly surprised; his personal plea about the mountains, from now onwards, he noted in the margins to the poem, will be: 'O let them be left, wildness and wet . . .'

After that he emphasized that line by simply italicizing it, and altered the word 'weeds' in the last line to 'streams', adding that he challenged his teacher, to whom he will send the altered version, to spot the error quickly. The original last line had been: 'Long live the weeds and the wilderness yet.'

His teacher, later, in an e-mail reply, was sharper than his student had thought he might be; he spotted the substitution immediately and added that August ought not to be a weed himself and mind too much about the transient additional presence on a mountain. In his experience you could still enjoy the illusion that you were the first to understand the mass and majesty of the high places.

What the electronic circuits have enabled, in this brief sketch, is a private discovery and a consequent private correspondence with a trusted teacher, who was himself, let us suppose, freed to spend the next day mailing responses, praise, support, encouragement, reproofs and the usual sarcastic rejoinders to each member of his class. Typing each reply took time, but time for the work had been created by having each class in the school work at home for one day of the week. Electronic writing's unlikeness to print gives it great scope as far as altering the original is concerned. Good students could become adept at weaving reader response and subjective first thoughts around the text, linking with arrows, circles and such like where necessary, but often the end-result of such visible musing is an altered original, a kind of negotiated 'best fit' between writer and reader which can draw upon the teacher as arbiter. The student re-writers can begin to scaffold their own creative work through this imitative kind of originality. Work by Wendy Lynch (1993) shows how well students are able to adapt poems once they have the original held in place and are able to retain the matrix for their own substitutions.

The third vignette was given as a way of exploring the possibility of writing in a certain mode becoming ever more private and individual, because the development of individuality will require as much wrestling with the difficult and previously unencountered, as reader or as writer, as anything conceived at present in orthodox English teaching. August's teacher, far from abandoning his class to the machines, has, in order to work as a supportive and useful presence, to understand each individual well, and be ready with further ideas for reading and with ideas which will provoke creative responses. The electronics could well help to encourage speculative and individual minds, for these are the kinds of people who do not necessarily find the social pressures of the classroom conducive to individuality. We are back to the idea that electronic texts allow more sophisticated kinds of individual provision. If they are allowed to, then this will be seen as problematic for the idea of standardized assessment, but it is the opposite side of the similar difficulty presented by collaborative work.

Assessment problems will become more acute when writing by students is less and less obviously their 'own' work in the sense that they originate, at the point of typing or penning, each of the words on the page or screen. Creativity for writers will, as Lanham (1993) points out, come to be as much a matter of re-combining existing elements, in physical as well as mental form, as starting afresh each time with a blank page. Given that all kinds of styles, varieties and rhetorical positions will become valid too, then standardizing will have become practically impossible. If what is happening in higher education at present is any guide to what will happen in schools in the future, then we can see that the time will come when any hope of covering more than a limited number of the total set of possibilities is recognized. Courses and their associated assessment will be modularized, and, before this process is complete, there will be some almighty rows about what will remain central and at the core, beyond the realms of modular choice. The conflict between the long established idea that the process of writing is something restricted to the individual and the claims for the recognition of other more 'collective' forms of writing, and the recognition given to individual contributions within them, will continue for some time, though work has already been done to develop our thinking in this area, seen, for example, in Styles (1989).

However, how the contribution of those individual writers is evidenced and understood will be the subject of new thinking. Pasting, collaging and re-casting existing texts will all be seen as evidence of authentic and individual thinking, though not by those who do not understand by what processes literacy changes. Eventually, though, the teachers will win the assessment fight, and assessing English in the future will be much more like assessing drama now; there will be local judgements made by teachers, moderated locally. 'Locally', however, will refer not to physical distance but to specialism and rhetorical realm.

When the students are able to draw upon a plenitude of references, electronic concordances on literary and non-literary databases, and the rest, then experts in particular fields will be required as moderators, partly to weed out plagiarism when it is presented as originality, but mainly to judge with what skill originals have been adapted or applied. There was an apt instance of this sort of critical acumen at work when Christopher Hitchens in 1995 heard President Clinton quoting Auden's 'In the deserts of the heart/Let the healing fountains start' following the Oklahoma bombing. Hitchens presumed that someone had found 'healing' in a 'computer keyword search', and that the discovery had 'evidently been enough to recommend this otherwise completely inapposite verse'. We do not imagine that too many candidates will model their efforts on presidential speech-writing, but Hitchens's critique points to the kinds of judgement which assessors will have to make about the use to which the found writing is put. The students themselves, at the composition stage, will also have to learn about apposite kinds of incorporation. There is, of course, a major teaching programme implied in all this, one which will become the responsibility of the English teachers, but which is bound up with a larger concern about understanding 'information' and its nature. Students need at present to be taught how to process, in their minds, and critique an 'informational' text, but thinking about the significance of such a programme for English brings us back to Green (1990) and then forward to the relationship of writing not just to reading, but to other forms associated with mixed media of a kind that can interlock and mutually inform in digitized text forms. That will be explored later in our final vignette.

We said above that English teachers will, in the future, win the battle for control of the assessment process. The victory by teachers over politicians' convictions about assessment will come at a time when significant numbers of parents have enjoyed an education which derived benefit from the use of information technology. In this context, the continued use, by the curriculum-controlling politicians, of the words 'pencils' and 'paper' will make audiences first giggle, then yawn. Speakers will realize that the ploy of invoking the cheap past as if it were an adequate substitute for the supposed deficiencies of the complex present will leave them looking like the only people in the room (or on the circuit) who still have personal secretaries; everyone else copes with the use of one technology or another.

Parents who manage a world in which messaging becomes more and more crucial, or at any rate more self-conscious, and where multiplying media create subtler distinctions of custom and purpose than ever before, will cease to mind quite what their children do with words and their interplay with sounds and pictures. All that will matter is that their children bring home learning profiles which demonstrate that they have been engaged, creatively and with understanding, in shaping an outcome through a text, whether in the material and social world or in the imagination of the 'readers'. Those working at their best will show engagement with a task involving creativity, wit, the exploration of form and the sustained intelligence both to create *ex nihilo* and to re-cast existing texts and images, often with a satirical, moral or critical intention. English will not lose its essential concern with criticality, but we have to envisage a future in which no one can any longer expect any one set, genre or privileged type to be the paradigm example of an assessable text.

A typical 'approved syllabus' in the future will show aspects of the kind of thinking that informed developments in coursework during the late 1980s.

Individuality will be manifested through a whole variety of means, such as: extracts of transcripts of phone calls made by one student as part of a team arranging a conference at their school (transcription easily performed following the introduction of 'voice processor' circuits into school machines); voice-over explanations on a documentary; poems to accompany the camera's images (on documentary or lyric themes); poems as projected sculptural holograms that change with the sunlight; statements about the historical and cultural signi-ficance of Mick Jagger, with quotes from video compilations; accounts, as a series of brief before-and-after film clips, with commentary, of how to improve the mother-and-baby facilities at a nearby hyper-warehouse; or a chapter from an epistolary novel made up of e-mail letters. In each of these examples, the original elements can be extracted from the group effort. In the last instance, the chapter may be written by two people, but if each consistently handles one side of the correspondence, they may claim credit for individual work. Writing the paired text could be popular with those who develop a good working rela-tionship with a pen-friend in another country, and it might help the promo-tion of an international baccalaureate in English. Immediately this happens, of course, widely different varieties of 'non-standard', non-British English will have to be validated.

At the basis of much of our thinking about the changed nature of assessment is the idea of an increasing number of text types. Simply to illustrate that there is already evidence of this coming about, we note that now, in a Leeds compre-hensive school, the students in English type in a phrase from their Shakespeare play, and then simply watch the scene containing that phrase being played back for them on the video disk linked to the computer. This is in 1996, so it is not at all absurd to conjecture that eventually a standard coursework assign-ment will be for students to produce multimedia texts made up, in part, of short extracts juxtaposed so as to enable comparison and to illustrate it. The recorded extracts could be linked together, on one reading, by the students' own critical commentaries and observations, but those critical commentaries might be as much about performance elements as thematic ones or purely about verbal aspects of the script, or they might tie them together: 'Watch how Olivier suddenly glances to the left here – what is he frightened of?'

To return to our three instanced and entirely fictional visions of literary studies in the future, what do they amount to in terms of electronic text? In each, the computers have been used to extend, in some way that catches the imagination of the users, activities which almost any English teacher might want to see happening. The programs enable extensions to the present forms of literary study, but only in the second of our three vignettes has the capacity of the computer to act in diverse ways been a problem; however, aspects of computer use will begin to cause questions about how the reader is positioned in relationship to literary texts in print and those same texts on screen.

Lanham speculates about, for example, the literature student who substitutes unusual type faces, on a simple selection, throughout the screen-based text of

*Paradise Lost.* 𝕲𝖔𝖉 becomes gothic in type and 𝐋𝐮𝐜𝐢𝐟𝐞𝐫 decidedly unthreatening and informal in San Francisco type. This example seems like a trivial game without a great deal to do with sophisticated critical response, but it does, however superficially, acknowledge that a post-Christian audience has problems with the representation of God and Satan which perhaps Milton's original audience did not have. Perhaps this typeface game could be developed into a proper series of questions, or perhaps other applications than a few word-processed substitutions could come into play in order to explore textual features and linguistic patterns. Every student can be a Caroline Spurgeon now, a counter of images and word frequencies, but they will have access to a very large number of kinds of text, and are likely, once they explore the applicability of a particular analytic tool, to test its capacities across several different kinds of text.

These could be from Kress's (1995) new trinity of types or from any other diverse set where interest could lie in cross-comparison. At one end of the ability range will be Professor Sutherland's (1994) 'new virtuosi of the virtual library', asking scholarly and well theorized questions about the differences and relationships between writers on any number of significant counts, but at the other end might be ordinary kids told to look out for stylistic signals of informality in TV soap scripts (terms of address, slang phrases, trendy word uses), who stumble across a digitally held corpus of spoken English and note with some glee that the paucity of swearing on the soap in question is one of the signs of its not being like life. This is so, they assert with a newly found respect for objectivity, because, according to Rundell (1995), the 'f' word is used 313 times per million spoken words by young speakers of both sexes, though not at all by middle-aged women. (But who can guess what kinds of changes will have occurred within the acceptable areas of the spoken language by the middle of the next century?) The soaps, they note, when challenged to do something worthwhile with their discovery, have got the ladies right, but not the youngsters.

This was a chance discovery on their part which came about because the corpus presented itself and threw up information about the 'f' word when one of the naughty youngsters typed it in and told the search engine to begin, anywhere. The teacher, upon noticing the class's unexpected interest in the corpus, then devised a few more games for them to play with it, including writing a story whose first line occurs from the list of phrases incorporating the speech device 'I goes', as in 'I goes, with Kelly? I don't talk to Kelly no more'; or from the list 'not exactly', as in 'not exactly how you wanna feel just before you get married' (Rundell, 1995). As Kress points out, it is not much use worrying about using standard English in our productive futures, and the capacity of the electronics to render our language back to ourselves is likely to sustain an interest in the actual rather than in some politicians' cultural preferences.

In any case, it could well be that placing literary and mundane writing on the same corpora of language, alongside daily speech, would enable a fusion of categories which are now separated, very often, at the level of analysis and study. It might seem a little odd that we speculate about young school students having access to scholarly databases written about in learned journals, but in fact there is nothing odd at all, given the existence of a schools version of the English Poetry Full Text Database, available from the publishers Chadwyck Healey at a fraction of its original cost, or the fact that the OED in CD-ROM form could be in most secondary schools before long (as well as the CD-ROM version of Johnson's dictionary). Students now are expected to read many historical texts, which have been edited with minute detail and academic care, and which come cheap in some paperback editions. The same thing will happen with digitally created texts, and so the future English teacher's job will grow, including within the scope of the content area the 'knowledge' to be taught, the use of digitally held texts as well as the revered printed books.

We need, now, to examine, by one last vignette, the kinds of teaching which will link non-literary texts to the abiding concerns of English with identity, experience and form. This vignette derives from Peter Medway's thinking about language and intervention in the affairs of the world (Brown *et al.*, 1990).

---

**This was Monday**

As Bill, one of the tiny handful of Williams to bear that nickname in 2040, the youngest English teacher in his department and its only male, struggled against a cross-wind riding his eco-bike to school, in the West Riding, that Monday morning, he felt renewed anxiety about how his class of 16- and 17-year-olds would ever finish the projects in which they were engaged. He'd been advised not to let too many experiments happen at once in his early days as a teacher, but the project had, luckily, proved interesting to almost everyone in the class. Different aspects of it had been taken up in different ways, but each with enthusiasm, so it had been hard to impose a uniform pace. The trouble was that it all had to be finished by Friday; that was in the plan, and the resources had to be available to other colleagues from that day.

What had fired the general enthusiasm was the reaction of the students to meeting, getting to know, working with and working for the war veterans from a special home next to the school. These people were national celebrities of a minor kind, being some of the last of those who had fought in the Gulf War, and who were now, in their seventies, in what was virtually a military hospice. Bill, who had graduated from Lincoln University in history and textual studies, had taken up an opportunity which seemed to him the purest good fortune. He had arranged contact between his class and a group of ten veterans. At first the students had been massively apprehensive, but the ground had been prepared by Bill, in that the class had met the chief nursing officer of the soldiers and one of the fittest and most reliably cheerful (for PR purposes) of the troops before they themselves had gone to visit The Hospital, as it was simply called. They had also practised some questions on Sgt Cheerful.

What the contact eventually led to was a diverse and rich set of conversations, explorations of documents, letters and messages on behalf of individuals, and the organizing of a collection of recorded spoken memories which the local archivist was later to show great interest in, all lasting over, merely, a ten week period. It was not all to be as positive and straightforward as that, however.

For example, Kiri and Nelson, the kinds of kids who took you to the edge as a young teacher, had cracked open a file of audio-visual material held by the Broadcasting Corporation of Iraq. 'Look what we've found, sir,' they'd cried. Bill had had to ensure that never again did any school machines accept Kiri and Nelson's file-breaking code, and the experience would have been even more unpleasant had not his head of department backed him all the way in a series of fast and furious electronic exchanges, via translator circuits which were far from perfected yet, with the Iraqi authorities, who were internationally famous for fussiness over copyright. The odd thing was, though, that once all the reassurances and apologies were accepted, the Iraqis forgot to ask if Kiri and Nelson had copied the file before returning it, which, of course, they had. They had then used the material to create some strange re-writing of received histories; they had cut and pasted images into a ten-minute video compilation entitled 'Look What a Good Boy Am I', which showed, complete with added music, using images borrowed from the unacknowledged Falklands War, that the rival war leaders all comported themselves in exactly the same way in front of troops; there was almost nothing to differentiate their body language.

Bill was bothered about the approach here; it was not the exuberance and iconoclasm which bothered him quite so much as the fact that this exercise had done nothing to connect the students to the people whom they were to work with, and for. Today they were to show their work to the veterans, about whose reactions he was apprehensive. He need not have been, however, because one of the veterans was on screen for quite long enough for his mates to recognize him, even after he'd spotted his younger self and stayed silent.

Meanwhile, Josiah and Bianca had responded well to the veteran assigned to them, had liked the old soldier and were led, following curiosity aroused by initial conversations, to look again at video-recordings (held on the files of the National Audio-Visual Library) of the Gulf War. At first this was to bring their own background knowledge up to scratch, but more and more the point of the looking (on the English Department National Library terminals) became an exploration of the gaps between the image of the kind of fighting suggested in the audio-visual archives, and the impression of the experience given by their veteran. They had discovered that the more they went back over the same questions to him, the less the original answers – which did seem to confirm the impressions given by the film makers – seemed to hold true. This they established fairly quickly because they could electronically superimpose one transcript on another, and see some key differences straight away. They had also discovered that it was no use appearing to ask the same questions time and again; that merely made their interlocutor impatient. As a result they had spent a long time working out how to get at the same issue via a different wording. There was a vast amount about that very art available on the circuits, said Bill, but he had told them to worry about that later, when they were 22. They were to worry now about the balance of their own writing against the video clips, and the distribution of that writing across their whole text.

This was Monday, and they had only until Friday (two doubles) to finish reports which they had entitled 'Legend and Experience'. A great deal would have to be done at home, but he'd have to ask Cheri, Head of Heritage, if they could skip Wednesday's session on the music hall. As a peace offering, he would give her class a local site on 'the death of soccer'. Josiah and Bianca's account took the form of a compilation of video interviews with their subject, edited footage of 1990s reportage from both film and newspaper sources (from the European News Schools' Data Bank), their own voices and a good deal of written text which sought essentially to interpret some of the preceding material. The picture that emerged so far from the compilation was of a man who had been no idealist in his youth, but who had been haunted by the terror of those he had helped to capture, and troubled even more by the misery of many of those 'released' from the terror of the earlier invader when allied troops entered Kuwait.

We weren't 'lions led by donkeys', he'd said, but had also asked if the kids could come up with a phrase like that which encapsulated how the ground troops stood in relation to those who'd sent them into the field. Bill was more taxed over the answer to this question, when his students put it back to him, than he was about any other issue in all his conversations with this pair of students. This was Monday, and he still had nothing satisfactory to offer. However, frustration about the answer to that question was blocking his thinking about how to get Bianca and Josiah to see in what ways their text needed editing. At present all the writing was in one section – was it not possible to re-distribute it, yet preserve its essential interpretive capacity? This was Monday . . .

Sheila was one of the few who had expressed outright displeasure at the prospect of meeting the veterans in the first place. In the event she endured, without overt rebellion, her teacher's demand to go there and talk to that quiet and slightly frail looking gentleman in the corner. Bill's intuition about character had been validated in the event and the outcome was that a man who wanted a letter writer found one who was good at the dying art of the hand-written letter.

When the history of English teaching up to 2070 comes to be written, in part as a tribute to Shayer's (1972) work up to 1970, what will it say about the advent of the great changes in approach and content that are likely? It would be tempting to reproduce a page or two as a way of finishing this chapter, but instead, let us try to summarize how things will be shaped, and thus speculate about what the history might include: how some sets of cultural, economic and technological forces will influence a subject which, quite properly, will remain a central one in the educational enterprise.

So far we have been discussing English as if it will remain a separate subject in the curriculum even if its subject matter ceases to be purely literary. However, it may well be, under pressure of mixed and merged media and in response to the richness of provision of textual types on the circuits, that, as suggested in Chapter 3, English will merge with, or incorporate, other areas, such as music and art. In recent years, teachers of English have been eclectic, borrowing methods and materials from other disciplines to illustrate, in an intuitive way initially, the process of meaning making in various genres, outside the purely language based. Yet at the same time other teachers have similarly been reaching into areas historically reserved for the English teacher. Both movements show every sign of accelerating further. Throughout this chapter is has been clear that distinctions between drama, media studies, communication studies, film studies and English are based more upon historical accident and curricular politics than they are upon the emerging shape of the area of study within which all of these subjects, and more, can be seen to fall. On the other hand, our analysis suggests that there can be no easy falling back upon the notion of the individual's personal exploration of his or her experience as an alternative, highly learner-centred model for curriculum structuring. What is required is far less clear, but perhaps the direction in which to look is towards a curriculum based, throughout compulsory schooling, upon a small number of widely defined curriculum areas, one of which would cover all the concerns with which this book deals.

Relationships between schools and the wider community are going to change, in that the new technologies will re-define where schooling takes place, and who provides it. Much of it will be out in at least the electronic dimension of the community, where the community itself will no longer be based in a single geographical locality, but comprise a shifting set of partially overlapping interest groups with which pupils are in contact through the new communications networks. Membership of these interest groups will in many cases not be delimited by nationality or age group. In those circumstances, the range of kinds of English that pupils encounter will widen significantly, as will the range of kinds of text.

Relationships between home and school need some exploration. At the moment it is easy to observe that those groups who, for the most part, are themselves most qualified, arrange happily enough for their children to be educated by systematic progress through syllabuses which sustain subject differentiation. Even if their sons and daughters have access to CD-ROMs and the Internet at home, there are few signs as yet that home–school distinctions are dissolving. Perhaps the relationship between home and school will change, but for radical change to occur we must conjecture the widespread social acceptance of home–school relationships outlined in the vignette about the student August, home-working for a day a week because his progress can be monitored and advanced via e-mail. Much depends upon social attitudes and social class; those who have, for generations in the United Kingdom, wanted their sons out of the way at boarding schools are unlikely suddenly to welcome them back home simply because they can work on a computer. At the other extreme of this frightening gulf, at the working-class community, or, more gloomily likely, at the unemployed and near zero-wage community level, where school attendance rates are not famously high except in rare pockets, it is hard to see how computer-based education will succeed where other forms have failed. Unless the youngsters perceive how more help can come through the machines than through school-based teachers, it is hard to be optimistic about educationally worthwhile experiences happening at home. Roszak (1994) notes how information technology's potential in helping the unemployed and the poor to find things out that will help their plight is an entirely lost potential, and, worse, deliberately so.

For information technology to play any significant role in establishing home as a compensatory environment in educational terms, some rapid development work will have to be put in hand, so that local economic communities can call upon the best that has been discovered so far in self-tuition materials. A difficulty might well be the limitations of the home itself, and so we have to speculate that, for security reasons, machines and software will have to be placed in the twenty-first-century equivalent of Carnegie libraries. These could be the places where different interests intersect, where individuals could discover how to join in wider communities, such as those envisaged above, sustained more by interest and other marks of identity and shared culture than income. Perhaps a twenty-first-century equivalent of Carnegie might like to start structuring such places in the least advantaged areas in our cities.

Relationships between schools will change. On one level this will be the result of what, unless steps are taken to prevent it, will be the widening technological and financial distance between the most active users of new technologies and the least. As the range of new technologies increases, the distance along this spectrum will increase steadily. Where individual schools come in the great cross-country new technology race will matter to them and their pupils. How the schools overall are distributed around the course (bunched at the front, or spread across the whole distance) will matter nationally and internationally. Another locus of change will be the growth of distance learning. In the university sector this has steadily expanded the geographical areas from which universities draw their students, and created new opportunities for both cooperation and competition as a result. The same will happen with schools, as it becomes possible for children to take all or some of their teaching from schools or further education colleges that are geographically distant. This will potentially benefit some schools and disadvantage others, in ways that will depend greatly upon the precise financial and regulatory framework that is evolved to manage these changes in the best long-term interests of all concerned. Once charging becomes common, quite new forms of commercial home tutoring over the Internet become a possibility too.

These changes will open up new possibilities for English teachers in particular, as their skills are widely valued internationally, and full-time distance teaching in Germany while still living in Wales, for example, may be the sort of opportunity that begins to open up. Questions about comparative rates of pay across the European Union will start to arise as a result.

The number of physical spaces in schools required for pupils will fall, other things being equal. To the extent that some learning can be conducted electronically, whether carried out by teachers from the pupil's own school or others, there will be less need for the amount of physical plant currently provided, as much of this electronically based work could be carried out at home. This suggests either that schools are only used for part of the week, or more plausibly that a smaller supply of places will be kept available for five or more days a week. These will be used for pupils individually attending for only part of that time, as tertiary level students do now. The internal design of schools will need a drastic rethinking in consequence.

The present balance between active and receptive learning will move significantly towards the latter. Similarly, the balance between individual and collaborative work will swing towards the latter too.

As a result of these other changes, control over the learning process will become more fragmented, as will control over the curriculum content actually encountered by the pupils, as distinct from formal control over what they are expected to learn, as specified in national curricula.

Perhaps our conceptions of what learners are like will change too. The use of new technologies will, according to Lanham (1993), allow young communicators to discover in which modes – writing or pictorial images – they are most at home. As this was being written, Michael Ignatieff, in a radio broadcast, suggested that 'anyone who thinks the computer . . . culture is leading us to barbarism should think of dyslexia. In a new age we can't afford to privilege literacy skills at the expense of visual and spatial ones. We all need the dyslexic imagination.' Digital technologies may well come to disrupt, among other things, previously stable sets of ideas about who are good learners and what needs to be learned. If once we were certain that the bright are universally adept and read and write well, and the not-bright compensate only in craft skills for their lack of literacy, then that view may not be so easily sustainable once the strugglers with reading and writing have turned their attentions to computers and communications. The mechanicals of *The Dream*, good joiners of wood but poor linkers of sentences, not-bright people who struggle with words and punctuation, manifest a deeply embedded cultural attitude which is likely to have influenced learners' views of themselves. From now onwards, though, messaging will be a craft skill too and the virtuosi will have more media at their command than words.

We do not know, of course, that disparate sets of forces will work together very well. English teaching, both in schools and in higher education, has a tendency to variety of form (see Barnes *et al.*, 1984). Nothing should lead us to believe that the tensions inherent within the subject will ease just because new purposes present themselves and because the current restraints might one day be lifted. Control over the learning process will become more fragmented, as will control over the curriculum content actually encountered by the pupils, and in the loss of these controls, communities of interest will have to establish new rhetorical positions, new alliances and definitions of where intellectual centres may be constructed.

First, we have to accept in working towards the new that, from now onwards, explicit attention must be given to features of text medium, type and use, along the kinds of lines indicated in the fourth vignette. What has been added to printed books, handwriting, typing, radio, television and telephones is a variety of devices which enhance these things, merge, extend, re-orient and (in Lanham's word) re-purpose them, and in so doing challenge some of our basic notions about the best ways in which to learn. In the sense that the new technologies compose a rich list of additions, then teaching life becomes more complex; there is greater real choice. Teachers will have to spend time ensuring that students grasp what kinds of enquiry are best suited to which medium, where the greatest satisfactions lie, for reading as an enjoyable activity, and where critical thinking and reflection ought to begin. English would inevitably thus come to embrace media studies as an integral part of what it did, not, as it were, alone for the benefit of raised cultural awareness, but because upon understanding of the media depends understanding of how best to learn.

Second, and with somewhat greater difficulty, we have to try to see how theoretical thinking about literary and language study will impact upon literacy studies at school level; and, third, how the technologies will tie in with the theories. In many ways this book has indicated how, in terms of re-casting the social roles of writer and reader, in changing the nature of texts and their relationship to traditional ideologies, and in bringing new text structures (Bolter, 1991) into play, theories of literacy practice and technology work well together. We would, though, also do well to see how very constant some forms of study have been in the UK, untouched by modernism or postmodernism and likely to remain untouched by digitized text, such as A level English literature.

There are other points where the technologies and the theories do not tend in the same direction, so that it becomes hard to envisage a future free from internal division and argument. Lanham's work, for all that it fascinates, does at times lean towards an almost romantic view of how the computers will grant insight and enable learning simply of themselves. There is a decidedly Rousseau-esque streak to be found in some writing about computers and learning. Advocates of change can seem to be so awe-struck by the technology that they see the students as innately able to fulfil its most virtuous uses; they are learners through being users of a technology which grants understanding simply by storing and presenting 'information'. The newest multimedia computers imply, to these same souls, by their mere availability as it were, that teachers have only to provide the hardware, watch the elegant ease with which the students learn its applications and then give them a theme to explore, whose outcomes will demonstrate that separate subjects are no longer tenable in the way they were in a print-dominated culture. Students will merge speech, music, images and readable verbal text, and the whole product will be a reflection of the free but collaborative imagination of the learners, whose acuity can be so much better evidenced through these new technologies than through writing.

Our quarrel with these Rousseau-esque visions is partly with the naiveté of their optimism, though not essentially with their trust in the students, but mainly with the damage which they could so easily do. Education could suffer badly in a future in which teachers were seen, by politicians, as dispensable, replaceable in effect by sufficient computers. English could well become more complex in a future that was rich in choice and generous with dilemmas, but only a determined imagination can sustain the balance of technologies and human minds. Anyone seriously interested in the degree of fine balance required in order to begin to evaluate the threat on the one hand and the promise on the other would do well to read Sven Birkerts's (1994) eloquent book, *The Gutenberg Elegies*, referred to in Chapter 2. The future of literacy is likely to be changed as much by such devices as the taped novel and the videoed adaptation as it is by the computer. In any imagined future, English teachers will have to continue to be critical leaders, people with a vision of what can be done by whom and of what is worthwhile.

Finally, we shall need to see how far the learning opportunities offered by the new technologies are taken up, utilized and extended. All societies are probably more interested in the end with what their children learn than how they learn it, and so in a sense what happens to methods of learning is of relatively small consequence. In any case there is, in general, a tendency to revert to the tried and tested whenever education is seen to be in a state of crisis, and it may well be that politicians of both the real right and the supposed left see to it that the rhetoric of crisis is maintained.

However, what if, in our imagined future, the electorate did finally tire of league tables and the idea that school is a once-only experience? If that happened, if something like life-long education became a genuinely popular enterprise, with a great deal of supported self-study routinely involved, then the adults, engaged with the means to learn, would start to want to know what their children were up to. That is when the big enquiries will begin, when adequate resources will be devoted to understanding both the possibilities and the blind alleys of the new and when twentieth-century educationists will be criticized for their timidity in failing to ask the right questions.

# Appendix 1: Members of the NCET Future Curriculum Working Group

| | |
|---|---|
| Anthony Adams | University of Cambridge |
| Hugh Betterton | Inspector for English, Sutton |
| Stephen Clarke | University of Leeds |
| Andrew Goodwyn | University of Reading |
| Gunther Kress | Institute of Education, London University |
| Hilary Minns | University of Warwick |
| Phil Moore | Independent consultant |
| Lucy Newlyn | St Edmund Hall, Oxford University |
| John O'Connor | Westminster College, Oxford |
| Peter Scrimshaw | Open University |
| Margaret Meek Spencer | Institute of Education, London University |
| Jane Spilsbury | NCET (seconded English and Media Studies teacher) |
| Jeremy Tweddle | University of Central England |
| Sally Tweddle | NCET |
| Shona Walton | Warwickshire LEA |
| Alastair West | Redbridge LEA |
| David Wray | University of Exeter |

# Appendix 2: Thirty-nine texts reviewed for the NCET's vision programme

Ball, D. and Foot, R. (1988) *Power for Young Mathematicians*, Coventry: NCET.

Ball, D., Higgs, J., Oldknow, A., Straker, A. and Wood, J. (1987) *Will Mathematics Count?* AUCBE.

Carter, R. (ed.) (1991) *Knowledge about Language and the Curriculum*, London: Hodder and Stoughton.

Courtois, G. (1992) Breakdown in education in Leonardo supplement, *Independent/ Le Monde et al.*, 152–4.

Department for Education (1991) *Education and Training for the 21st Century*, London: HMSO.

Employment Department (1990) *1990s: the Skills Decade; Strategic Guidance on Training and Enterprise*, Sheffield: Employment Department.

Ennals, R. and Cotterell, A. (1985) *Fifth Generation Computers: Their Implications for Further Education*, FEU.

Finegold, D., Keep, E., Milibrand, D., Raffe, D., Spours, K. and Young, M., (1990) *British Baccalaureate*, Institute for Public Policy Research.

Fisher, P. (1990) *Education 2000: Mixing Educational Change with Consent*, London: Cassell.

Forester, T. (1989) *Computers in the Human Context: Information Technology, Productivity and People*, Oxford: Blackwell.

Griffin, J.A. and Davies, S. (1990) Information technology in the national curriculum, *Journal of Computer Assisted Learning*, 6, 255–64.

Handy, C. (1991) *Age of Unreason*, London: Arrow.

Hawkridge, D. and Vincent, T. (1992) *Learning Difficulties and Computers: Access to the Curriculum*, Kingsley.

Holt, J. (1976) *Instead of Education*, Harmondsworth: Penguin.

Keeling, R. and Whiteman, S. (1989) *Education 2010*, Newman Software.

Kinsman, F. (1991) *Millennium: towards Tomorrow's Society*, Harmondsworth: Penguin.

Lawlor, S. (1990) *Teachers Mistaught: Training in Theories or Education in Subjects?* Centre for Policy Studies.

Lyman, P. (1991) Library of the (not-so-distant) future, *Change*, Jan./Feb., 34–41.

Martyn, J.,Victers, P. and Feeney, M. (1990) *Information UK2000*, Bowker-Saur.

Meek, M. (1990) *On Being Literate*, London: Bodley Head.

Microelectronics Education Programme (1986) *CALL for the Computer*, CET.

Miles, I., Rush, H., Turner, K. and Bessant, J. (1992) *Information Horizons: the Long Term Social Implications of New Information Technologies*, Aldershot: Elgar.

Moore, N. and Steele, J. (1992) *Information Intensive Britain*, Policy Studies Institute.

Northcott, J. (1991) *Britain in 2010*, Policy Studies Institute.

NCET (1992) *New Technologies in Schools in the UK*, EEC.

NCET (1989) *Turtling without Tears*, NCET.

(1992) Nouveaux gestes de le micro-informatique, *Science et vie micro*, 96, 66–70.

Richardson, T. (1992) Implications of new educational technologies: accommodation and systems in the next 5–10 years (private circulation).

Royal Society of Arts (1992) *Electronic Education: Its Role in a Learning Society*, RSA.

Roszak, T. (1986) *Cult of Information: the Folklore of Computers and the True Art of Thinking*, Lutterworth Press.

SEAC (1992) *Assessment of Performance in Design and Technology*, SEAC.

Shuard, H. *et al.* (1993) *Forward 2000: Integrating Logo into Primary Mathematics*, Harlow: Longman/Logotron.

Toffler, A. (1973) *Future Shock*, London: Pan.

Toffler, A. (1992) *Powershift: Knowledge, Wealth and Violence in the 21st Century*, New York: Bantam Books.

Tweddle, S. (1992) Understanding a new literacy, *English in Education*, 26(2), 46–53.

Vocational Education and Training Task Force (1989) *Towards a Skills Revolution*, CBI.

Watson, D.M. (1992) The impact report: an evaluation of the impact of information technology on children's achievements, Department for Education (private circulation).

Weizenbaum, J. (1976) *Computer Power and Human Reason: from Judgement to Calculation*, Harmondsworth: Penguin.

Williams, S. (1985) *A Job to Live*, Harmondsworth: Penguin.

# Appendix 3: Background reading for the Future Curriculum for English seminar, November 1993

Adams, A. (1990) Distance support for student writing through electronic mailing, *Australian Journal of Remedial Education*, 22(3), 28–31.

Adams, A. (1993) A language for Europe: using a computer-based simulation in initial teacher education, unpublished paper

Kaplan, N. (1992) Ideology, technology and the future of writing instruction, in *Evolving Perspectives on Computers and Composition Studies: Questions for the 1990s*, Urbana, Illinois: National Council for Teachers of English.

Kenny, J. (1993) Liberating the imagination: taking hold of information, in *Developing English: Approaches with Information Technology*, Sheffield: NATE.

Kress, G. (1993) An English curriculum for the future, paper presented to the National Association of Advisors in English Annual Conference, Durham, January.

Moore, P. (1992) Authoring – an educational perspective, unpublished paper.

NCET (1993) *The Future Curriculum with Information Technology*, Coventry:NCET.

Neelands, J. (1993) *Drama and Information Technology: Discovering the Human Dimension*, Coventry: NCET.

Tweddle, S. (1992) Understanding a new literacy, *English in Education*, 26(2).

Tweddle, S. and Moore, P. (1994) Working within a new literacy, in S. Brindley (ed.) *Teaching English*, Milton Keynes: Open University.

Tweddle, S. and Moore, P. (1994) English under pressure: back to basics, *Computers and Composition*, 11, 283–293.

Wood, D. (1993) *The Classroom of 2015*, London: National Commission on Education.

# Bibliography

Andrews, R. (1996) Visual literacy in question, *20:20*, 4.

Barnes, D. and Barnes, D. with Clarke, S. (1984) *Versions of English*, London: Heinemann.

Barthes, R. (1977) *Image, Music, Text*, London: Fontana.

Birkerts, S. (1994) *The Gutenberg Elegies: the Fate of Reading in the Electronic Age*, London: Faber and Faber.

Bolter, J. (1991) *Writing Space: the Computer, Hypertext and the History of Writing*, Hillsdale, NJ: Lawrence Erlbaum.

Brine, J. (1991) The implicit power of educational technology: word processing and collaborative publishing at the primary level, in I. Goodson and J.M. Mangan (eds) *Computers, Classrooms and Culture: Studies in the Use of Computers for Classroom Learning*, London, Ontario: RUCCUS University of Western Ontario.

Brown, J., Clarke, S., Medway, P., Stibbs, A. with Andrews, R. (1990) *Report of the Project: Developing English for TVEI*, Leeds: University of Leeds/The Training Agency.

Buckingham, D. and Sefton-Green, J. (1993) Making sense of the media from reading to culture, *English in Education*, 27(2): 1–10.

Cameron, D. (1990) *The Feminist Critique of Language*, London: Routledge.

Chandler, D. and Marcus, S. (1985) *Computers and Literacy*, Milton Keynes: Open University Press.

DES (1984) *Curriculum Matters 1: English*, London: HMSO.

Dias, P. and Hayhoe, M. (1988) *Developing Response to Poetry*, Milton Keynes: Open University Press.

Eklundh, K. (1994) Linear and nonlinear strategies in computer based writing, *Computers and Composition*, 11.

Eraut, M. and Hoyles, C. (1989) Groupwork with computers, Journal of Computer Assisted Learning, 5, 26.

Fairclough, N. (1989) *Language and Power*, Harlow: Longman.

Fothergill, R. (1981) *Microelectronics Education Programme: the Strategy*, London: DES.

Fowler, M. (1994) Whose fantasy should we teach? How children use their understanding of media and new technologies in their writing, *The English and Media Magazine*, 30: 25–31.

Goodwyn, I. (1992) *English Teaching and Media Education*, Buckingham: Open University Press.

Graddol, D. and Boyd-Barrett, O. (eds) (1994) *Media Texts: Authors and Readers*, Clevedon: Multilingual Matters.

Graves, D. (1983) *Writing: Teachers and Children at Their Work*, London: Heinemann.

Green, B. (1990) A dividing practice: 'literature', English teaching and cultural politics, in I. Goodson and P. Medway (eds) *Bringing English to Order: the History and Politics of a School Subject*, Lewes: Falmer Press.

Hannam, C. (1965) A lesson in Henbury, *New Education*, 1(14): 11–13.

Hills, P. (ed.) (1981) *The Future of the Printed Word*, Milton Keynes: Open University Press.

Holmes, B. (1997) A cross-cultural comparison of the use of computers in British and Japanese classrooms, PhD dissertation, University of Cambridge.

Iser, W. (1978) *The Act of Reading*, London: Johns Hopkins University Press.

Jones, J. (1995) *Shakespeare at Work*, Oxford: Clarendon Press.

Keep, R. (1991) *On-line: Electronic Mail in the Curriculum*, Coventry: NCET.

Kress, G. (1995) *Writing the Future: English and the Making of a Culture of Innovation*, Sheffield: NATE.

Lanham, R. (1993) *The Electronic Word: Democracy, Technology and the Arts*, Chicago: University of Chicago Press.

Leach, S. (1992) *Shakespeare in the Classroom*, Buckingham: Open University Press.

Lynch, W. (1993) The role of the classroom computer in the promotion and development of literacy, MEd dissertation, University of Leeds.

Masterman, L. (1980) *Teaching about Television*, London: Macmillan.

Masterman, L. (1985) *Teaching the Media*, London: Routledge.

McMahon, H. and O'Neill, B. (1993) A story about storying, in M. Monteith (ed.) *Computers and Language*, Oxford: Intellect Books.

Monteith, M. (ed.) (1993) *Computers and Language*, Oxford: Intellect Books.

Moore, P. (1994) Authoring, *English and Education*, 28(3): 11–14.

Norman, K. (1992) *Thinking Voices*, London: Hodder and Stoughton.

Robinson, Bernadette (1993) Communicating through computers in the classroom, in P. Scrimshaw, *op. cit.* (1993a).

Robinson, Brent (1985) *Microcomputers and the Language Arts*, Milton Keynes: Open University Press.

Robinson, Brent (1993) in M. Monteith, *op. cit.*

Rosenblatt, L. (1938) *Literature as Exploration*, New York: Modern Languages Association.

Rosenblatt, L. (1978) *The Reader, The Text, The Poem: The Transactional Theory of the Literary Work*, Carbondale: Southern Illinois University Press.

Roszak, T. (1994) *The Cult of Information*, 2nd edn, London: University of California Press.

Rundell, M. (1995) The word on the street, *English Today*, 11(3).

Scrimshaw, P. (ed.) (1993a) *Language, Classrooms and Computers*, London: Routledge.

Scrimshaw, P. (1993b) Reading, writing and hypertext, in P. Scrimshaw, *op. cit.* (1993a).

Shayer, D. (1972) *The Teaching of English in Schools, 1900–1970*, London: Routledge and Kegan Paul.

Stibbs, A. (1991) *Reading Narrative as Literature: Signs of Life*, Buckingham: Open University Press.

Styles, M. (ed.) (1989) *Collaboration and Writing*, Milton Keynes: Open University Press.

Sutherland, J. (1994) When in ROM, *London Review of Books*, 16 November.

Taylor, N. (1994) The films of *Hamlet*, in A. Davies and S. Wells (eds) *Shakespeare and the Moving Image*, Cambridge: Cambridge University Press.

Tilbury, D. and Turner, K. (1996) Levels of understanding: the case of acid rain, *Teaching Geography*, 21(3): 118–21.

Tulasiewicz, W. and Adams, A. (1997) *Teaching the Mother Tongue in a Multicultural Europe*, London: Cassell.

Tuman, M. (1992) *Word Perfect: Literacy in the Computer Age*, London: Falmer Press.

Turkle, S. (1996) *Life on the Screen: Identity in the Age of the Internet*, London: Weidenfeld and Nicolson.

Wegerif, R., Collins, J. and Scrimshaw, P. (1996) *CD-ROMs in Primary Schools: an Independent Evaluation*, Coventry: NCET.

Wilkinson, A. (1971) *The Foundations of Language*, Oxford: Oxford University Press.

Williams, R. (1981) *Culture*, London: Fontana.

# Index

# SIMULATIONS IN ENGLISH TEACHING

## Paul Bambrough

Simulations allow the exploration of processes and environments which would not otherwise be accessible in the classroom. These might be real world environments or processes, such as a town planning meeting, or fantasy scenarios. Students take on roles and function within these simulated environments to explore both how the world they have entered operates and how they can best function themselves to achieve given objectives in that environment. Simulations are experiential – participants learn by doing. Participants in role feel able to take risks, to fail as well as succeed, and they can look back at and learn from their experience after the event.

Paul Bambrough has applied simulations to the English classroom to allow students to explore language use in social/functional contexts other than those usually experienced, and to enable the exploration of literary texts by allowing students to enter the world of the text.

This book includes sections on simulation design (including a major section on the design of a simulation for working with a text) and using simulations, combining theoretical and practical approaches. No prior knowledge of simulations is assumed, and this is a valuable introduction for all English teachers.

### Contents
*An introduction to simulations – Designing simualtions for English teaching – Designing a simulation – Running the simulation – The debrief – The language experience – Issues of control and reality – References – Index.*

112pp     0 335 19151 7 (Paperback)